Up or Down, Right or Wrong

is

IRRELEVANT

By

John Pierre LeCedre

Copyright © 2023 by: JohnPierre LeCedre

For a question, a comment, or a request, you can reach the author at this email address:

jlecedre@yahoo.com

Request your **FREE e-book** copy of this book or any other book by this author from Amazon <u>during the promotion periods</u>. You will receive an email from the author notifying you when a book is promoted for free.

DEDICATION

We are all connected... in a pool of humanity. While one has little effect on the whole, the whole greatly affects everyone. A pool that reflects our human needs, desires, wants, and aspirations. At times, we become too extended between our fear and greed. What might start with ripples, develops into waves and tides that reach every part of this pool. Only humans make the market... And humans become the elements of the market, the participants in a seemingly endless expression of their humanity...

I share my thoughts and experience in this book with those who are, directly or indirectly, market participants... With all the passion that we share and being a part of this free market system...

I thank you from the heart...

My sincere gratitude,

John Pierre LeCedre

RISK DISCLOSURE

DISCLAIMER

This book is written solely for informational purposes. The author is not any of the following: a broker, a financial planner, a money manager, a security dealer, a trading advisor, or any other financial professional stated or not stated in this disclaimer. This book is sold with the understanding that the author expresses only his personal ideas and opinions as an individual investor and a trader. The author does not engage or render any financial, accounting, legal, or any other professional services such as trading, investing, or managing other people's accounts, or give advice or make any recommendations. He only manages and trades his own account. If any of these services are needed, readers should seek professional help and advice from their certified professionals.

No ideas or opinions or statements in this book should be considered as a recommendation, advice, or solicitation to buy or sell any kind of securities. The author has no affiliations with any securities dealers or brokerage firms or mutual fund families. Any securities' names or symbols used in this book are used only for demonstration purposes, expressing the author's personal ideas and opinions. The author does not guarantee or warrant that readers who

V

choose to use the author's system described in this book will achieve profitable results.

Readers should understand that financial markets are always changing to reflect all the changes in the economy, politics, national and international events, and an unlimited number of possible events which may vary the degree of risk described in this book. Therefore, the author disclaims any responsibility for any unfavorable results that might arise directly or indirectly from using this personal system described in this book.

Readers should also understand the potential risk involved in trading any market before they attempt to trade. By purchasing this book, the readers agree not to hold the author responsible or legally liable for any matter that relates to this information. This book is sold with the understanding and the agreement that it is only the readers' responsibility to assume all consequences of their trading. Like any other system, the system described in this book involves certain risks and may not show results similar to those shown. Readers should look at the information available in this book as an additional and different tool within their hands to deal with the market using their own judgment.

TABLE OF CONTENTS

INTRODUCTION

Have you heard that the world is going digital? Of course, you have, and if you have not, just look around you, and you will see almost everything is going somehow digital. Maybe you are wearing a digital watch, using a word processor, balancing your checkbook with an electronic device, buying gas from a gas station, accessing your bank account, etc. There is an endless list of digital applications in our lives.

The irony in all that is the real physical world is anything but digital. The world moves in a continuous manner and not in increments, unlike what these technical instruments seem to suggest. We try to quantify almost everything into flowing numbers. Why do we need those digits to process simple things like time or filling a gas tank? The answer is obvious and simple: numbers yield clear and more objective results and make things easier to measure. Nevertheless, if you look around you, you will notice that the real physical world is analog (continuous) and not digital (steps) at all.

Look at the sun, for example. Oh, just kidding! I know you cannot look at the sun directly with your naked eyes, but you can see the sunlight during the daytime. You will notice that the sun does not seem to be moving in steps but in a very unnoticeable continuous manner as it appears to our eyes. Of course, the sun is not moving; it's the earth, which is rotating around itself one turn every 24 hours. You will also realize that it's almost impossible to accurately tell time this way (minutes and seconds) because the earth does not seem to be moving at all at any particular moment. Actually, the earth is rotating around itself at 1670 km per hour (about 1040 miles per hour) near the equator. Yet we don't feel the rotation of the earth because the speed is constant, and we are held to the earth's surface by gravity. Nevertheless, sunset and sunrise are real proof that the earth has been rotating. Our day and night are an indication that one full rotation has already occurred, and another day cycle has been added to the count of days.

Well, since the sun can blind our eyes and the day cycle is just 24 hours, let's look at something slower without the need to deal with the brightness of the sun. Look at the lawn in your yard, for example! Have you ever wondered how much your grass grows every time you mow it? Maybe you mow a few inches of your grass every couple of weeks.

Yet, if you try to observe this growth with your eyes for several minutes, you will get tired and bored, and you would not see any growth at all with your eyes. The reason is that the grass is growing continuously and seemingly at a very slow rate to be detected by human eyes in a few minutes. But still, when you come to mow it in a couple of weeks, you would see its growth in inches.

You maybe are wondering why does it really matter if the analog (continuous motion) world is treated digitally (changing in steps) or not? How does that relate to the financial market? Going back to our time example, you may realize that you cannot tell the exact minute or second by just watching the rotational motion of the earth around itself and relative to the sun. Neither you can see your grass growing in your yard at any particular moment in time while you are watching it until a certain number of days would have passed by already.

Let's see how that does relate to the market. The market is also an analog entity, like everything in the real world. You cannot see how it will move until the move is done, like in our examples with time and grass. While the earth rotates at a constant speed and always in the same direction, and a healthy lawn always grows provided it's well maintained and watered, such events are accurately predictable. Unlike the rotation of the earth and the growth of the lawn, the financial market's moves are completely unpredictable because these moves can be up, down, and sideways with varying speeds.

You certainly know during a nice shiny day in a stable weather environment that a beautiful sunset on the horizon is coming followed by a dark night before the sunrise appears again on a new day. Such events can be predicted very accurately to the minute. We know that because the earth always rotates in the same direction at a constant speed. You also know that you can plan to mow your lawn at specific periods because the lawn's growth is very predictable. However, it's extremely difficult to predict the market's moves because the market continues to move in different directions with variable speeds, making it impossible to predict its moves accurately.

Therefore, you cannot tell by watching the market how the market will move next, up, down, or sideways until the move is done. That happens because there is no precise and repeated order in market's moves. Furthermore, once a particular move is done, it becomes useless information in terms of any future predictive power. Such a move in the market becomes simply stored historical data. While this data can tell you where the market has been and what it has done, it can tell you nothing about the future direction of the market and what it would do next.

Some of the readers might strongly disagree with me here with such a conclusion, arguing that technical and fundamental analyses provides a very powerful means of predicting where the market is going. I know such tools are very popular among traders and money managers in dealing with the financial market. During my 29 years in the market, I had much faith in these tools to realize later on after painful losses that they are of little value. I will certainly address this subject later on in this book. For now, I rather just say one thing: if you are looking at one piece of information that many other market participants are looking at, that information is basically obsolete in terms of future predictability use. Such information has been already discounted by the market and is reflected in the price. While knowledge of the market is very useful to understand the rules of the game and mitigate your risk better, this knowledge does not give you much of any future predictability.

About 75 to 85% of money managers of several thousand mutual funds underperform the market every year. That is not a coincidental matter, but a persistent statistical fact year after year. And to make things worse, the 15 to 25% that outperforms the market in one year, often underperforms the following year. As they say, even a broken clock is right twice per 24 hours, that's 8.3% of the time! These money managers are very intelligent and highly educated from prestigious schools. They have the best tools they need to make their decisions regarding their investments and the market direction. Yet, no one can outsmart the market by predicting the direction of the next move in the market, except usually by luck.

Think about it, if all it takes is a PhD from Harvard or Yale or any other prestigious business school, all those individuals with PhDs in finance and economy will be very rich individuals. However, most of these people end up often being college professors with comfortable lifestyles, but certainly not very rich people. In other words, they earn their living by telling other people how to make money. But why a well-knowledgeable person cannot predict the next move in the market? Simply, the knowledgeable person cannot know how other market participants will react at any particular moment in the market.

For those of my readers who were involved in the financial market in the 1990s, as was my case, you might remember our famous then-Federal Reserve Board Chairman Alan Greenspan and his famous phrase "irrational exuberance" describing the stock market in December 1996. The Nasdaq was trading around 1500 at that time. Nevertheless, three years later, the Nasdaq reached the 5000 mark! What can be more powerful than the chairman of the Federal Reserve and his board of directors in influencing the market? They have every financial tool in their hands and the power and knowledge of setting monetary policies. They oversee the economy and influence the interest rate. Every word uttered by the chairman of the Federal Reserve can drastically move the market up or down. Yet, even such a powerful individual was way off about the market direction. So long for all those people who claim they can predict the market. Nobody can, period.

Now, the obvious question that comes to the mind of most of the readers of this book is: if no one can predict the market direction correctly and if almost everyone, in the long run, underperforms the market and fails to predict the next move correctly in the market why should I, the author of this book, think that I can? The answer is: I cannot as well! Then you might be wondering why should you read this book.

Like everyone else, I cannot predict the next move in the market, and I don't even try to do that. I really don't know where the market will move next; it could be up, down, or sideways. Of course, I have my own opinion about the market, like most people. I might inject some fundamental and technical approaches, but that is just my opinion. My opinion is just an opinion; it does not matter one way or another. I can be very wrong, like everyone else. This is the beauty of this market system, which I designed and decided to call the Digital Market Machine System, or (DMMS) for short. The market direction is truly irrelevant. That is the difference between all those gurus out there and me. Simply, I don't forecast, predict, or bet on one direction in the market, period! To do otherwise is simply guessing, speculating, and pure gambling. Definitely, I am not a gambler.

This book views the market as an analog entity. The system shown in this book attempts at digitizing the market's moves. As hard as it is to know the exact time in terms of minutes and seconds just by looking at how the earth is rotating around itself relative to the sun, it's quite easy to tell the time accurately if you have a digital watch. Throughout this book, I will provide you with all the needed details and explain step-by-step how to apply DMMS in the market. My sincere hope for all those who take the time to understand the materials thoroughly will be rewarded financially and emotionally in the long run. They will be able to sleep well at night and worry less about whether it is a bull or a bear out there pushing the market in one direction or another. They would smile when they hear that someone is trying to predict the direction of the market by projecting his opinion and making bets on its outcome, knowing that investing is much more than just a guessing game. Guessing in the market is just gambling in the biggest casino in the world.

CHAPTER 1

WE PRETEND TO INVEST WHEN WE'RE GAMBLING

There is a clear distinction between an investor, a trader, and a gambler. If someone, for example, uses his money to develop a hospital or a factory, we may conclude that this person is an investor. Such an investor provides a useful service or a product to others, and he or she expects a reasonable return on his or her original investment. Similarly, if someone buys food products from farmers and sells them to consumers, we may conclude as well that this person is a merchant or a trader. The trader buys the merchandise with the intention to sell it back relatively in a short time at a higher price in order to realize a profit. The trader in this case also provides a valuable service to others by facilitating the process of marketing and distribution between producers and consumers.

Finally, if someone enjoys gambling in a casino, we may rightfully conclude that he or she is a gambler. The gambler certainly does not provide much of a service or a product to others, except maybe recycling back his or her money in the economy. In this case, the casino gets the money and provides jobs to its employees and entertainment to its customers. Winning or losing money reflects a deep emotional need for one's personal satisfaction in dealing with risk.

In the financial market, this clear distinction becomes very vague among market participants. There is a very fine line between an investor, a trader, and a gambler in relation to the market. In fact, even this fine line seems to become more blurry and disappears altogether at times when dealing with the financial market. Even a buy-and-hold investor buys a stock with one intention that the stock price will appreciate further. A trader buys a stock with the intention to sell it soon, hoping to make a quick profit. As for the gambler, he might not even bother with the shares. He might just buy a call option on the stock, risking his entire original investment spent on the cost of the option for the thrill of making much more.

Clearly, each one of these people has his or her own way of making money with the stock. Nevertheless, all these people are doing a similar thing but in a different way, betting that the stock will go up. Otherwise, all of them lose money in this case. That distinction between investing, trading, and gambling becomes very blurry. Anyone of these people would feel justified to say that he's "investing" in the market, "trading" the market, or "betting" on the market. The reality is, all these people are gambling when they bet on an outcome in the market, regardless which way is done.

Does it really make much difference if you bet on an up or down market than betting on a black or red position on the roulette table or on the dice outcome on a craps table? There is not much difference except the name of the game and possibly the time people take to execute a trade in the market or a bet in the casino. We usually use a more socially acceptable label in the market, such as "investing" instead of "gambling", though we are doing very much the same thing.

Those readers who spend quite a bit of time doing some research on a particular investment and apply their technical or fundamental analysis, or a combination of the two, may object to comparing investing to gambling. I objected too in the past when I started dealing with the market. I do admit that investing does involve a great deal of research to reach a decision regarding an investment, in comparison to making a bet almost blindly on a casino table. Fundamental analysis such as supply and demand, P/E ratio, book value, etc. Or technical analysis such as chart patterns, a trend, support, resistance, etc. with numerous indicators that many traders swear by them that they have considerable influence on the outcome of an investment.

While gamblers can make their bets in the casino almost blindly on games that are just pure luck, traders make considerably more effort in searching and analyzing their trades. That is true, however, since most traders do the same thing, the additional effort cancels each other in the market. If you are looking at the same thing that other traders are looking at, how can you have any advantage over the others? By the time you get the information, it's already too late. The market is so efficient, and it reacts so fast to reflect any new information in the price. What you know has already been discounted by the market, and you are left where you started, wondering what will be the next move in the market, hoping that it will continue in your desired direction.

That may sound very contradictory to everything we learned about traditional investing rules that we may have learned in schools or heard from professional people. Simply put it this way: if all it takes few fundamental figures such price to earning ratio, book value, etc., or studying the chart pattern of securities, most people would be rich. Not to underestimate education, but there are plenty of nerds in the world that are willing to learn every little detail and apply it to the market, and hence, everyone becomes rich, right? Wrong!!

Most of these figures or chart patterns tell us what happened in the past, and that by no means is an indication of what to expect in the future. When we trade a stock or any other financial security, we trade them from the right side of the chart, not the left side. The left side of the chart is the past, the history of the individual security's moves. The right side is the unknown side because it's still a part of the future. As far as I know, no human being has the supernatural ability to predict the future. We just guess; guessing is gambling unless the odds are very high on your side. This is the purpose of this book, which is to give you very high odds when you decide to make a move in the market. Don't believe anyone who claims to be able to predict the future. Every time we enter a trade, we are faced with the same three outcomes: up, down, or sideways. The risk of a sideways market is the loss of time and any potential profit. If options are used, the loss can be up to 100% of the premium paid for an option if the price does not go into the money.

Strong fundamental data and a well-defined uptrend of a stock don't guarantee that the trend will continue after you get in the trade. Remember, this information has already been discounted by the market. The stock might continue its uptrend if the company can still produce unexpectedly excellent performance. But even in this case, some market participants start selling on the excellent news, thinking that cannot be sustained. Don't be surprised to see the stock has reached its peak and started to decline even with the best news. Most likely, the stock price has been pressured by high expectations and trading at a hefty price causing some shareholders to lock their gains by selling.

Buying a stock at a high price certainly cannot produce profit unless the price of the stock moves higher. Some traders buy high-flying stocks, thinking that it's more probable that the trend will continue higher. This is called momentum trading. But once a stock loses its momentum, the decline will be steep and fast, and you will end up with devastating losses. So, should you buy a stock trading at a low price? The answer is NO! A low price is not always an indication of a good deal. The company is maybe performing very poorly for whatever reason and will continue to decline. You will never recover if you get yourself in such a trade. A low-priced stock can still go lower to pennies and stop trading altogether. Yes, that happens to many companies on their deathbeds. I am sure you heard of many well-known big companies that went out of existence. Do you remember Sears and Kmart? They don't exist anymore!

Whatever the price might be, low or high, that price reflects the value of that stock at that particular time, and that's all it is worth. The problem seems to be always the same: what's next? Up, down, or sideways? We try to guess the next move in one direction based on what we already know, then place our bets, risking our principal and worrying about the outcome. Is that any different from placing a bet on a roulette or craps table, hoping the ball or the pair of dice outcome would match our desired outcome? Now that is gambling to my understanding.

But what about all the millionaires made by betting on Microsoft, Coca-Cola, Apple, and other hot and popular stocks? Some people wonder. Many of these people might not realize how many other stocks go to zero or never take off, leaving frustration and disappointment with great losses that no one talks about. Sure, we mostly hear about the few successes, because failures, often, are ignored. When people play the popular lottery game, no one with a reasonable mind expects to win the jackpot of several hundreds of millions of dollars. Nevertheless, lottery players don't mind spending a few dollars taking a shot, hoping they would beat the odds against them and realize their dreams. When the winning number is drawn randomly, people and the media talk only about the prize winner. All other players who lost their few-dollar bets are ignored.

Nevertheless, when people "invest", they take their investments very seriously, not like betting a few dollars on a lottery game that they can spare a few dollars to lose. They are risking their hard-earned money. They cannot afford to lose their "lifeblood and sweat". Likewise, they truly think, as they have been taught and trained, that it is the right thing to do to ensure a good financial future for themselves and their families. These people think of themselves as "investors" instead of gamblers; so they don't want to lose their capitals. Whether these market participants do or don't understand what they are doing, does not change the reality of the market. As it's the case with every crowd, mass psychology always leads to one extreme or another, as defined by fear and greed on the human emotional spectrum.

The problem always remains the same: Our inability to predict the outcome of a particular trade in the future. We keep using past data and chart patterns and indicators to help us foresee the next move. But most market participants are looking at the same financial data, the same chart patterns, and the same indicators we are looking at. How can this approach give us any advantage in terms of future use when what we know is just common knowledge already reflected in the price?

This approach is basically useless in terms of future use. However, I don't discard technical and fundamental analyses. I use them mostly to sense how other market participants think and feel about a particular investment. Besides, these analyses can tell a lot about the past, the present, and the mass psychology of the market crowd.

But how about all those popular gurus out there giving their forecasts and opinions about the market and promoted by the media? Isn't it worth taking their advice and recommendations? Many of these gurus make their money by telling other people how to make money. Their main objective is to prescribe new individuals to their market newsletters for a monthly fee, so you can receive their recommendations. Nothing is wrong in charging people for the effort and the expertise of an experienced individual who is providing his service to guide and help others, as long as he puts his own money where his mouth is. That is, he would be acting on his own recommendations as well.

I admit some individuals are far more experienced and wise than the majority of the people involved in the financial markets. They understand the risk/reward ratio better and how to process the most fundamental, technical, and various political and economical news. Nevertheless, most of these "experts" underperform the market! As a matter of fact, market sentiment is often measured by the number of bulls and bears within this category of experts. Ironically, studies show that the market goes the opposite way to what the majority of these expert individuals predict. Are you surprised? Theoretically, this indicator should be bullish if the majority of these experts are bullish. Nevertheless, the market usually declines when the bullishness of these experts is excessive. Similarly, the market advances when there is excessive bearishness within this category of experts. What does that tell you? Ironically, this indicator is more useful as a contrarian indicator to predict major turning points in market direction.

Even individuals with strong influence on the market cannot predict the market. The chairman of the Federal Reserve of the United States is the most powerful person in terms of financial influence and monetary policies. In fact, he's the most powerful individual in the world in this regard, since the US Dollars is the reserve currency of the world. Words uttered by the chairman of the Federal Reserve can send the financial markets around the world in a wild move, up or down. Some of us might remember a good example to that during 1990s. By the end of 1996, Dow Jones was trading at around 6000 up from about 3000 in 1993. Similarly, the Nasdaq was trading at about 1200 up from 600 for the same period.   Alan Greenspan, the chairman of the Federal Reserve at that time, made his famous remark regarding "the irrational exuberance" describing the fast upward move in the financial market. That famous remark was intended to slow the market down. Nevertheless, the Dow continued its move upward to 12000 from 6000 between the end of 1996 and early Year 2000. The Nasdaq went up wildly from 1200 to 5100 in the same period, about 3.5 years. That's about 4.5 times! See Figure 1.1

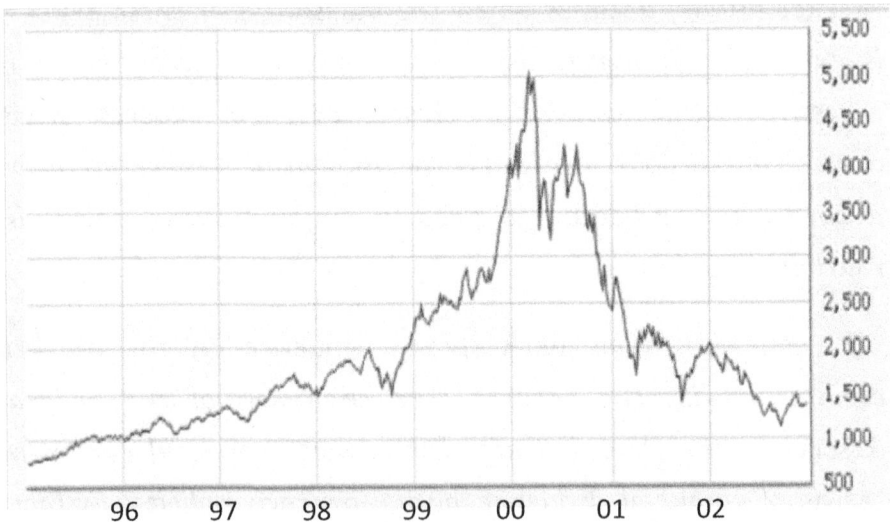

Figure 1.1 NASDAQ during the dot.com 2000

How could the most influential man in the world be so wrong on the market direction? How could the Chairman of the Federal Reserve with the interest rate stick in his hand be so much off? Yes, the market does what the market wants to do, regardless of what anyone thinks. Isn't this good proof that no one can predict the market? Yes, no one, everything is just speculation.

You may or may not know that 75 to 85% of money managers of mutual funds underperform the market annually. At the time of writing this book in the Year 2023, we have about 8000 mutual funds while we have about 5000 stocks in the market. Yes, there are more mutual funds than stocks! Does that tell you something? What makes it worse is most of the 15 to 25% outperforming in a particular year, they underperform the following year. One might wonder how much of that is just luck instead of genuine performance. Remember! Even a broken clock can be right twice a day. These fund managers are highly educated and equipped with the best tools and assistance to do their market research and analysis. Yet the same statistics persist year after year. Why is it so difficult to predict the next move in the market? Like the Chairman of the Federal Reserve, these money managers have access to everything they need to make the right move. Nevertheless, the results are far off!

To assume that tracking the earning record of a company or watching its stock's chart will tell you its future move, would prove later on to be a deceptive and deceiving assumption. Who said that the market is a logical place anyway? For example, a company's earnings might be showing losses quarter after quarter, yet its stock price might jump up at the last earning report just because the loss was less! Another example is a company that is showing excellent profit quarter after quarter, its stock price might decline sharply at the last earning report. This decline happens just because its earnings did not increase enough or missed the expectation by a few pennies! That seems the most illogical thing. Of course, the market often moves on expectation, not only on performance.

Mass psychology dictates the direction of the market, ruled only by greed and fear. Have you ever looked in the sky and seen a bunch of birds flying together? Did you notice how they follow each other, then reverse their direction instantaneously without discussing their next move? Can you explain why when a few birds land or fly away, the rest of the birds follow? Or have you looked deep in the water to see a bunch of fish swimming together, then all of them change their direction immediately? What makes such creatures behave as a mass?

Market participants have very similar characteristics. The masses have the tendency to join the trend mostly at its end after the few and the most influential ones start the trend. The masses buy at the top because they see everyone is buying. Then they sell at the bottom as everyone throws the towel and sells. Nothing is special about that. It's just typical behavior of the masses in the market. As time goes by, trends are formed. One may wonder: how did I miss the trend? It always seems very easy to trade when you look on the left side of a chart. But this is the past, and it's history at that moment. Real trading is trying to guess the future and its unknown from the right side of a chart. It's always that moment when you stop and wonder, what's next: Up? Down? Sideways? You don't know and nobody knows; the guessing game continues.

The next thing that may come to mind is why not just follow the trend? By the way, that's the most popular way of trading. You see so-called "experts" in technical analysis drawing lines and locating supports and resistances on the chart and predicting the next moves, only to be disappointed later on. If all it takes is to learn how to draw lines on the charts, we would be all rich. So what would happen if we follow the trend? You often hear "the trend is your friend", right? The problem with this approach is, by the time you see the trend formed, it might be very close to its end. So you end up buying at the top or selling at the bottom, good luck with that. I say that sarcastically because it's a very painful thing to lose your hard-earned money trying to follow some of these predictions by "experts" promoted by the media.

Besides, the market never moves straight up or straight down; it fluctuates regardless of the trend and fools everyone. Normal fluctuations are to be expected and that can be tolerated, but when the market starts taking wild swings in both directions, that would throw most trend followers on the sideline suffering considerable losses from the resulting whipsaws. So the trend line might not be that much "friendly" after all.

One may wonder why not in this case trade the market as a contrarian? The answer to that is if you cannot be sure of what would the trend be, and where will be heading, how can you be sure of the opposite? I don't think the trend is always your friend; otherwise, it should let you know when it's about to change. A trend is just past history, and nothing can say that a trend will continue after you initiate a trade in the market. If all it takes is following a trend, then most people would learn how to draw trend lines and become rich.

Is it possible that everyone who invests in the financial market can become rich? Of course not, otherwise how all these rich people are going to get paid? Money is not going to come from the blue sky or nowhere. It's a game with a sum equal to zero. In other words, when one makes a dollar, someone else would be losing that dollar. This lost dollar goes to the winner. Therefore, it's impossible for everyone to become rich. Losers must exist in order to pay the winners, in order for the sum to be always zero. Realistically, the few and well-informed individuals or groups who know how to navigate the market, make fortunes in the market. These fortunes are paid to the winners by the many who naively think that they are investing for the long term.

As shown, we intend or pretend unconsciously to invest when we are truly gambling, yes, making bets on a certain outcome in the market. Sometimes the trend persists, especially in a bull market, and many people feel richer. Well, virtually richer, because real gains count only when one opens a trade and later on closes it. While the market is advancing, most people feel richer because they are bidding up prices. But the true winners are the ones who get very early in and head to the door first at the top to make a real gain. Those who get in and out late in the game, simply pay the ones who get in and out first. Believe me, that sucks!

There is a great truth in the market I learned through the years:

THE MARKET IS ALWAYS IN A STATE OF EQUILIBRIUM UNTIL THIS EQUILIBRIUM IS DISTURBED; THEN THE MARKET TENDS TO REACT IMMEDIATELY TO REACH ITS EQUILIBRIUM STATE AGAIN.

Not to change the subject, but I find myself again writing about equilibrium in this book. I wrote about the state of equilibrium in my book "Does God Exist?" showing that everything is always in a state of equilibrium or trying to reach an equilibrium state once equilibrium is disturbed. While everything is in a state of equilibrium or trying to regain its equilibrium, nothing can be in a "Perfect Order" state by itself. So an intelligent being must exist when complexity increases in the system. Check that book if you are struggling with your spirituality, it's not a religious book at all, but a logical and scientific approach to the question of God's existence. You can read more about this book in the "Other Books by This Author" Section.

But we are dealing here with the financial market, so we continue our discussion about the market only. One may argue, if the statement about the market being in equilibrium, why does the market fluctuate? Different market forces are pulling in one direction or another. Have you ever looked at the movements of a pendulum? Did you notice how it fluctuates from one end to the other end until it loses all its energy and stops at the equilibrium point in the middle? When a piece of news concerning the market is released, this equilibrium is disturbed. Then the market immediately reacts to reach a new state of equilibrium at a lower or higher level, depending on how market's forces are impacted by the news.

The market forces acting upon it can create wild fluctuations until that energy is dissipated in the market and a new equilibrium has been reached. If the market is closed when the news is announced, the market will gap up or down at its opening the following trading day. Simply, if you are not in it already, you will get in at the end of the move, and leaves you again with the same question: what's next? Up? Down? Sideways? Since the market already reached its new equilibrium state, you're again in the same situation trying to guess the future move in the market. Not helpful at all! You feel like tiny dust in the air pushed in all directions with every market move, hoping the market goes your way. Isn't that gambling when you keep speculating on the outcome of the market? But since the market is always in a state of equilibrium or in the process of regaining its state of equilibrium, you will be always guessing how the market will move next. Now that's gambling, when we are guessing the outcome of the market and making a bet on it.

Let us go of our way and assume the impossible to be possible. Yes, let's assume we can have access to any future news while other people cannot. (silly assumption, isn't it?) Of course, that is not possible, but let's pretend it's possible. So now you can have access to particular news before anyone else can. How can that help you? If you think that would help you guess correctly the right move in the market, think again! This will not help you either. The reason is different people react differently to the same news. Some market participants consider the good news as a buying opportunity, while others consider that an opportunity to sell at a high price. Yes, many sell on good news. I am sure you heard the expression "buy on rumors and sell on facts". This is why it's so difficult to predict the next move in the market, even when you have access to the news ahead of time. You don't know how other market participants will react to the same news.

This is why also Federal Reserve Chairman Greenspan was wrong on the market direction, even when he thought it was "irrational exuberance". That also explains why all those top-notch people with PhDs from those prestigious schools can be as wrong, too. That's why the ultimate majority of money managers underperform the market because It's impossible to know how millions of investors will react. Some of them are highly sophisticated individuals with great reasoning. But the market has all types of investors along the investing spectrum, from the highly informed to those not well informed enough. Everyone is creating his/her impact on the outcome of the market.

Yes, the market can go down on very good news, too. The logic behind that is some traders think it's an excellent opportunity to sell at a high price and lock their profits. Other traders might think it's better to wait and ride the trend. There is no way to know how the masses collectively will react to particular news and what the outcome will be, regardless of how knowledgeable or ignorant a person can be. Have you ever sailed on a boat in the ocean? You will notice the tiny ripples all over the surface of the ocean. Then you would see some larger waves formed. I will talk more about this concept later on as I discuss the cycles. But for now, imagine all those tiny ripples are the impact of each participant in the market. The larger waves are formed as those tiny ripples collectively combine their energy to produce those large waves. These large waves represent the trend in the market when more market participants pull in one direction than the other direction.

Now you can see why it's impossible to know the next move in the market, even if you have the knowledge and access to the news. You still have no control over how other market participants will react. The market becomes less predictable and less logical, representing only the net force of the masses collectively. This is mass psychology which dictates the market direction. Do you remember the birds and the fish we talked about? Humans behave this way too in many aspects of their lives, including politics, fashion, religion, and the market too. This is the herd mentality of simply following each other when something is popular or in trend. This is how trends are formed in everything. Regardless of what the media or other professionals tell you trying to explain a market move, by the time you see what the market has done, it's already a past event and useless information in terms of predicting the next move. It would take its place on the left side of the chart.

As you can see from our discussion above, logical reasons and research may help in understanding the past, but cannot really help much in forecasting the next moves. When the market becomes a part of your life as you become familiar with its behaviors, you would start to see many things that many people cannot see. I almost laugh when I hear a journalist on the nightly news explaining why the market dropped or advanced on a particular day. Nothing is wrong in reporting the financial news, but when opinions start to be injected into that reporting, that becomes nothing more than opinions and personal bias. The market in reality spends the whole trading day going up and down several times and settles at the end somewhere within that range. The funny part is you are given the same reason whether it ends up or down. Great reasoning and very helpful, right? Just being sarcastic, it's better for the news media to report the news without injecting their opinionated explanations.

Then you hear if you want to invest in the market, you should do your homework. Great advice! But what homework are they talking about? If you are a student, and you do your homework, you can get a straight "A". If every student does the same, it's possible that every student will earn an "A". In that case, it's better if the teacher grades the students on the curve. If everyone gets an "A", that's average! The average cannot be graded as an "A". So the test must be harder to introduce more competition and produce excellent results. Anyway, when it comes to investors, what kind of homework should be suggested? Does that imply that all investors can become rich? This is not how the financial market works. Some must pay for the others. "All" becoming rich is not possible. This is a game with a sum equals to zero.

Do you really think if you look at what everyone else is looking at is going to make you a fortune? Searching for a good company with a good earning, low P/E, below book value, strong sale, etc. cannot by itself give you a window into the future to foresee the move of the company's stock. This is what all business and finance schools teach their students. You cannot be ahead of others when you're doing the same thing others are doing. Others are looking at the same data you are looking at. So how can that give you any advantage over other investors when everyone is doing nothing more than what everyone else is doing? This is just "average"; average does not give you any advantage over others.

You might be wondering what investing has to do with others. You are just investing your money, and you wish the best of luck to everyone. That's a noble thought! Have you been in a class or an event where everyone gets the same reward and appraisal regardless of performance? While that might seem ok for some of us, to encourage kids or some people with low self-esteem, this is not how the real world is and certainly, this is not how the market operates.

The data you are looking at is already reflected in the stock price since everyone is looking at the same thing. This "homework" certainly will not get you the good results you're hoping for. How many times a company can report great earnings, but its stock loses a good chunk of its value just for missing the analysts' estimate by a few pennies? Yes, the market moves more on expectations instead of facts. By the time the facts are in, the move is already done. So knowing these facts ahead of time, assuming that is possible, still does not help you in better predicting the next move. Certainly, these facts are useless in future terms after the move is done.

As I said previously, the reason why one cannot tell how a particular stock or a market will move even when one can have access to the news ahead of time is that one cannot tell how other market participants are going to react to that particular news or facts. Otherwise, all these economists with PhDs and these securities analysts would be rich by now, but they are not. That is simply because most market participants don't view or react the same way as the logical and knowledgeable ones do.

That should explain why most gurus are wrong in the end, even though their reasoning is very logical and appealing. The problem remains the same: not everyone in the market has the same reasoning and the same reaction to pull the market one way or another. The masses' reaction would always have an element of randomness and chaotic characteristics that would make it very difficult for any well-informed and logical individual to figure out the outcome of all the combined forces acting on the market.

Remember those little ripples in the ocean while you're sailing, there is so much randomness and chaos until the collective net forces start to develop larger waves.

One may wonder, in that case, whether the market moves randomly. I certainly don't prescribe to the market random theory. Just because we cannot tell how the market will move next, that does not necessarily mean that the market moves randomly. Contrary to the dice on a craps table, or the ball of a Roulette game which have no memory of the previous history, the market feels, remembers, and does whatever it does for a good reason. Whether the market moves up or down, it's irrelevant. The market is trying to do one thing, trying to regain its equilibrium once it's disturbed. Once that equilibrium is reached, the market stays there with minimum fluctuations until that equilibrium is disturbed again by unknown events. The same process repeats until a new equilibrium level is found.

Think of the market as a little speck of dust in the air. When little or no wind is present, the dust fluctuates very little because it is in a resting position. That corresponds to low volatility in the market when there are no sudden or major events disturbing the market. However, when a strong wind blows, that little speck of dust moves violently in the direction of the wind, not randomly, creating a sizeable move in that direction. That corresponds to a strong trend in the market and certainly blows away the argument of any random theory that some people claim. Nevertheless, when the wind blows in different directions, the speck of dust moves violently following the same changing directions within a certain range. That corresponds to a very volatile and undecided market.

Why not then try to find out how the wind will blow the next time? The weather forecasters do that all the time. They are right very often, but not all the time. That might not be good enough in forecasting the weather, but that might be good enough in the financial market. Economists try as well to forecast the economy for the short and long terms, with less successful results than weather forecasters. There are many more changing variables when it comes to predicting the economy and the financial market. True, you don't need to be right all the time to make money in the market. Better yet, you don't even need to be as often correct as the weather forecasters, and you will still make money.

However, there is a difference: weather forecasters predict something is going to happen based on current real objective measurable variables in the atmosphere such as temperature, pressure, humidity, wind, etc. On the other hand, using fundamental and technical data to find out in which direction the wind will move the market is almost useless. The market has already discounted all these data. Everything you know has already happened. If you know something, most likely it is common knowledge between market participants and the move already took place.

Let's assume for the sake of this argument that you know something that no one knows. You still cannot predict the direction of the market. But why? The pool of the logical and reasoning market participants is much smaller than the less logical and less reasoning participants. So, even if you are an economist with PhD, you have no control whatsoever over how other people with less knowledge are going to react in the market. Remember, even the Chairman of the Federal Reserve failed to predict the financial market correctly. Most likely, you and I would fail this task as well. It takes more than logic and knowledge to be right on the market; it takes a strong wind, a force. Only the masses can supply this force which moves the market in a particular direction. Regardless of how knowledgeable an individual is, the average person cannot influence the masses one way or another.

Influential individuals such as the Chairman of the Federal Reserve, the Treasury Secretary, and other high-ranking politicians or well-known gurus might have a very temporary and limited effect on the market. But the greatest influence on the masses comes from the media as some journalists start injecting their opinionated views and expertise. In other words, instead of the media reporting objectively the news, the media starts to make the news using its influence and bias. Manipulated news can be of help only to those who generate the news. These individuals place their bets ahead of time and use the media to supply the force needed to move that particular stock up or down.

The average investor jumps on the wagon very late, regardless of how early one tries. Consequently, such an investor ends up buying at the top or selling at the bottom. After the strong move generated by the media is done, those who made a fortune on the move exit first. Then a counter move starts, and the masses start panicking on the way to the exit with great losses. You rarely hear about the losses of the many, but most likely you often hear about the fortune made by the few. You often hear about the big, successful companies that everyone likes to have some shares in them; but you rarely hear about the numerous stocks of the small companies that go to pennies or stop trading altogether.

If trend lines and good earning reports cannot guarantee future moves, you may wonder what else a small investor should do. The next chapter should go further in explaining why technical and fundamental analyzes are not enough to make money in the market.

CHAPTER 2

WHY NO ONE CAN PREDICT THE MARKET?

Can anyone predict the market? The answer is a big NO unless you believe in the supernatural abilities of some people who can overcome the time dimension and predict the future. Certainly, not many people have such abilities, if any. If the market were a linear entity, it would be very easy to predict the next move at any point in time. Even if the market were not linear but cyclical, then predicting the next move would be very easy as well, assuming these are accurate and repeated cycles. An accurate and repeated cycle, like our examples at the beginning of this book, the rotation of our earth or the growth of the yard's lawn would be very easy to foresee at any point in time as well. But the market exhibits several human elements with great variations.

Every market participant has his/her own views with a varied degree of opinion, understanding, logic, emotions, and actions. Therefore, it's impossible to become a predictable entity. If all market participants have the same views, logic, opinions, emotions, and actions, then the market can become predictable. However, remember, the pool of those highly logical and well-informed is much smaller than the pool of the not-so-highly logical and well-informed. These great varieties of market participants introduce these chaotic characteristics in the market, which makes it very difficult to predict its outcome at any time.

Nevertheless, many people who are participants in the market strongly believe that technical and fundamental analyzes are very helpful in navigating the market. They may argue that one can see where the market is going by analyzing price and volume charts or a series of earnings in addition to many other indicators. In fact, these approaches are very popular in the financial market and are used extensively by professional money managers, brokers, and individual investors.

I don't discard these financial tools when I want to take a look at what has been happening in the market. I do consider this type of analysis a reflection of what the market has been doing in the past. However, none of that has any predictive features that lead to the correct next move in the market beyond an educated guess. Such financial tools can be quite sophisticated and very impressive in helping money managers to influence other less sophisticated investors in adopting their views and taking their recommendations. In other words, these tools can be used as marketing tools to sell their financial products to generate fees and commissions.

Most likely, anyone who has some exposure to the market has heard that commonly repeated and legally necessary warning in the financial market to make this risk disclosure to investors: "Past performance does not guarantee future results". What does that mean? It implies it's a guessing game, though it's an informed guess. Just because the chart of the stock shows an uptrend and the underlying company produced good earnings in the past, there is nothing that says the same will continue in the future. In fact, a particular stock or market always moves on expectations instead of facts, which implies that the price itself is the leading indicator in terms of time. Therefore, by the time the facts are in, most likely it's time to take profit and head for an exit unless the expectations keep getting better for future performance.

As shown, a particular stock leads the underlying company and the general market leads the general economy, respectively. That is why the financial market can be considered an excellent future indicator for the economy since it is a leading indicator. Now one may wonder, how can the news of the economy be used to predict future market moves when the economy itself lags behind the market? That certainly proves the fallacy of any predictive features in arguing the usefulness of these analyses in any future terms, except guessing of course.

Most professionals and individual investors are directly or indirectly momentum players, as they assume the trend will continue to go up if it is up (or will continue to go down for short sellers). A similar assumption is made regarding earnings. If that is true, the trend in price and earnings should never change and all of us will be rich if all it takes is to find a trend and ride that trend. Unfortunately, it's not that simple and this is not reality. A trend can reverse at any time, regardless of how little or extended the trend has been.

This presumed continuity in a trend is a false assumption and deceptive sense of security. The disastrous decline of the heavy technology Nasdaq (-81%) during the dot com in 2002 and the financial meltdown of 2008 caused by the collapse of the housing market are good examples of the deception of riding the trend. At the time of writing this book (2022, 2023), we are having a very hot housing market again, and guess what! History is repeating itself. Buyers are afraid to miss the trend, so they buy at hefty prices, assuming the trend will continue to go higher.

Again this presumed continuity in a trend can be very disastrous if it happens that you buy your house or market shares at their peaks. You might not recover for many years if a steep decline follows. Of course, sometimes a trend feeds on itself. When the price goes higher, people assume that it will go even higher, attracting more buyers and pushing prices even higher. That can last for a while, creating a very extended trend for no valid fundamental reason at all except that more buyers are drawn to the bidding game with the expectation that the price will go even higher beyond any reasonable valuation.

We all heard the expression "buy low and sell high", but as the market becomes more speculative in an extended uptrend, a new philosophy emerges, "buy high and sell higher". It is that time when almost everyone becomes convinced that there is nothing that can take the market down. Unfortunately (or fortunately for those who sell at the right time), this game ends up being very painful for those who buy at the top when the bubble finally bursts. I already mentioned the disastrous decline of the dot com (2001) and the financial meltdown caused by the collapse of the housing market (2008) not long ago. Similarly, a downtrend can gain even more momentum since markets' declines are faster than their advances. This happens as market participants start to panic about the decline and rush to the exit at the same time. The decline accelerates as the short sellers come into the picture as they see the newly formed downtrend forming.

At any moment in time, the next move in the market is not any easier to predict than the previous moment. Whether you are a day trader, a short-term trader, or a long-term trader, it makes no difference when it comes to predicting the next move. Trading the market from the right side of the chart is in the unknown zone regardless if this is in terms of minutes, days, weeks, or even months.

Most trend followers insist that following the trend is the best way to trade the market. "The trend is your friend", didn't we hear that so many times? That is very true if you are lucky enough to catch a trend early enough and ride it all the way to the end and exit at the right time, assuming that you know exactly when the trend begins and ends. In fact, that would be the ideal thing to do. Nevertheless, real life is not ideal, and neither the market is.

Investors, most of the time, join the trend very late. To follow a trend, you need to see a trend, right? By the time you see the trend, you already missed a great part of it. Similarly, by the time you wait to see a reverse in the trend to convince you to exit your positions, most of your profit disappears, and you end up likely in the red losing a chunk of your capital.

Furthermore, some investors try to jump back on the trend wagon when they see the market rebounding in an attempt to recover some of their previous losses, they end up whipsawed by the market volatility adding more losses to their previous losses. They find out on their own that there is nothing friendly about a trend. It's simply a great marketing tool for professionals in the market to sell their opinions and recommendations to less experienced investors.

You can trust a friend because you can predict how a friend behaves. I doubt we can say that about a trend. Every next move continues to face the same guessing question: will it be up? Down? Or sideways?

Presumed continuity in a trend, more than often, can lead to great disappointment and sizable losses. If your broker might have told you that you can always protect yourself with a limit-stop loss, watch what would happen to your stock on a day when the underlying company does not meet the expectation of the market. And if the disappointing news comes after the close of the market, expect to lose a big chunk of the stock value at the open. What do you think would happen to your stop loss if your stock gaps down at the open? The answer is nothing; it would be ignored, and you are still holding the bag. Only market orders are executed in a fast-moving market. You would end up panicking and trying to sell at any price or keep holding it hoping for a rebound. If your stock is a blue chip company, you have a good chance of recovering some of what you lost after a long time. However, if you hold a stock in one of those small companies which usually have a short life expectancy, good luck to you. This would be one of the many valuable lessons you would learn in dealing with the market.

Looking on the left side of the price chart of a particular market or individual security can be very deceptive, sometimes by giving a false sense of the next move. If the trend is up on the chart, one may say "it's going up". This is certainly a false statement. In reality, the price has already gone up. One cannot tell whether it will continue to go up. Certainly, for those professional people in the market who tell people what to buy and when to buy, such wording "going up" helps them sell their services and recommendations to other people who need guidance in the market.

Think about it, isn't it much easier for a broker or a financial advisor when making recommendations to their clients, for example, to say "it's going up" instead of saying "it has gone up"? Using the progressive tense "ing" in "going up" is much more helpful in convincing their clients to act on their recommendations instead of using the perfect tense "has gone up". This is a powerful marketing tool that is very popular in the financial market environment. I should mention that most of these professional people are genuinely sincere in helping their clients. But like everyone else in the market, they too are convinced the presumed continuity in a trend is the best way to trade the market.

For this reason, most traders place their bets in the same direction as the trend. Financial advisors and brokers also make their recommendations this well too. Think about it! It would be extremely difficult for any guru or a broker to stick his neck against the trend. Most of these professionals go with the trend because it's much easier and safer for their business practice. If they are correct, they take full credit by patting themselves on the shoulders. When they are wrong, no harm would be done because almost everyone else is wrong as well. They cannot be blamed much for following the trend like everyone else.

There is a lot of risk in going against the trend, besides the financial loss. Credibility and reputation are of great value in this field for these professional people. Imagine a broker is calling you to convince you to sell a stock because he thinks your stock has topped out. Suppose you would follow his advice and sell your stock. If the price of that stock continues to climb, you would be quite resentful toward that wrong advice, and you might get rid of your broker as well. So, following the trend is the most popular and safest way to deal with the market.

When the market goes up, everyone would be cheering "it's going up"; and when the market goes down, everyone starts yelling "it's going down". Regardless of which way the market goes, you would hear someone in the media or somewhere else saying something similar to "I told you so" giving you all kinds of reasons and explanations why the market has done what has done. The only problem with this is their predictions are not predictions at all. The market was not going up or was not going down; the market has already gone up or has already gone down. They are only repeating what the market has done and not predicting anything.

Predicting implies describing a certain event that will happen in the future. Most so-called "predictions" are just guessing or describing events that have already happened in the market. How can that be called a prediction when it's lagging behind the market event? So the next time you see the market is up, and you hear someone saying "it's going up", or you see the market is down, and you hear "it's going down", smile! You are one of the few who still view the market rationally and wisely. You would know at that time, the market is already up and may not be going next any higher or the market is already down and may not be going next any lower.

Basically, you don't know and no one else does know the next move in the market. The advantage you have is at least you know that you don't know what will be the next move in the market. You become wiser when you don't just follow the crowd and jump on the wagon like everyone else. The next move is just a guess, a flip of a coin, and sadly a gamble of hard-earned money. If you are in the market to gamble, then it's your choice. However, you should not be gambling when you think you are investing.

Even a good earning report cannot be a good predictive tool to predict the future price of a particular stock. Some might wonder how a stock price can go down when the underlying company is profitable? The answer is simple: A stock does not necessarily move on earnings itself, but on the direction of earnings, that is future expectations. When the earnings of a particular company are reported, only better or worse than the expected earnings generate a strong move up or down. Even on a good earning report, shareholders might dump the stock if there is any hint that future earnings would be topping out or slowing down. Some stocks start going up even while the underlying company is not profitable at all if its losses are shown to be less than expected and its performance is improving. Hence, as you can see, it is more the direction of the earnings and the expectation of the investors that influences the behaviors of their stock prices.

If you are an active trader or an investor who is interested in technical analysis, most likely you have good knowledge or at least you often heard of most of the technical terms used in the financial market. Terms like a trend, trend-line, support, resistance, volume, moving averages, stochastic, macd, rate of change, relative strength, oscillators, on balance volume, envelope, etc. are just a few to name many more technical indicators out there. You may also be familiar with the many chart patterns such as head-and-shoulders, multiple tops or bottoms, triangles, rectangles, saucers, diamonds, flags, different types of gaps, selling and buying climaxes, and many more.

However, if you are not familiar with these terms, please don't be discouraged. You don't need technical analysis and the knowledge of using these terms or indicators to use my system in this book. There are plenty of technical analysis books out there if that is of your interest. As I said earlier, technical analysis is not a prerequisite for my system. The only reason I am mentioning them here is that some readers are interested in this approach. My point here is that indicators and chart patterns often don't necessarily lead to profitable trading, and certainly not much help in predicting the next move in the market.

Most market research and investment decisions are based on two types of analyses: fundamental and technical analyses. The fundamental analysis concerns itself with companies' values by looking at book values, price-to-earning ratios, current assets, future earnings, dividends, etc. Fundamental analysis has always been very popular in the financial market. Technical analysis has gained momentum and became extremely popular among professional money managers and traders. Short-term trading is mainly involved in technical analysis. Technicians and traders pay little or no attention to fundamental analysis. They do believe that all fundamental reasons are already reflected in the price, so why bother with that? They assume that previous price changes are strongly related to future price changes. As a result of these assumptions, a technician would recognize a price chart pattern on the left side of a chart and would try to predict the outcome of the price in the future based on past patterns.

I already listed some of these chart patterns above. Many books were written about technical analysis that can explain this subject in detail. These books classify these chart patterns into bullish and bearish categories, showing the most probable outcome of every chart pattern. Certainly, this is not the objective of this book. Interested readers who are interested in technical analysis, can consult other books regarding this matter. The objective of this book is to introduce a new approach to investing, a new methodology to deal with the market without being too concerned about the direction of the market. The system in this book looks at the market as a "business" instead of a "casino" by eliminating the "guessing" factor from investing.

Let's start first with the price itself since what we trade after all is price, not patterns, indicators, earnings, etc. What is the price anyway? We may say, what one is willing to pay someone else to buy something, a product or service, and both buyer and seller agree on a certain value. It is what both, the buyer and the seller, perceive to be the fair value at a particular time and certain conditions. In a market, where many participants are in the game of buying and selling, price becomes the result of that continuous struggle in defining the fair value between the bulls, the bears, and the undecided ones. The bulls want to buy at the lowest possible price, expecting the price to move higher. The bears want to sell at the highest price possible, expecting the price to move lower. As you can see, each side is speculating on the next move of the price. Then some participants start to switch sides in that struggle, which causes prices to swing one way or another as they switch between bulls and bears.

The net result of that struggle between market forces is what we call price, a perceived value, or consensus between all these struggling participants in defining a value of a particular security at a particular time. Nevertheless, such a value keeps changing with time as more or fewer participants enter the game and market conditions change. As more unknown factors become known, equilibrium becomes disturbed. The price reached in a previous moment, which was perceived to be a fair value, becomes a disturbed value. That is, the price becomes overvalued or undervalued, depending on the continuously changing perceptions and expectations of market participants. If such factors have little or no influence, that is they have been already reflected by the price and discounted by the market, little change occurs in the price. In such a stable state, the price fluctuates slightly around its equilibrium as the market perceives that price as the newly established fair value.

However, when sudden and unexpected events or unknown factors reach the market participants, that equilibrium reached earlier immediately gets disturbed. Price moves violently in a very short time as bulls or bears switch sides, creating a new net force balance where a new equilibrium level is reached by price and perceived as the new fair value. Such a reaction can be well demonstrated using the analogy of breaking a glass container full of water. Water, initially, is still remaining in that container. As soon as the container breaks for whatever reason, water rushes out immediately of the broken glass with a violent motion to settle in the surroundings where a new equilibrium can be found in a new and different shape container.

Such price changes are not just random movements. These price movements can persist in one direction or another for a while, creating rallies and declines. These rallies and declines develop as the result of intense emotional influence on the market due to mass psychology. Price moves up as more money is poured into the market as buyers become greedier and short sellers become too fearful as they are forced to buy back to recover their short positions, pushing prices even higher. This condition continues until buyers become more concerned about a very extended price level. As buyers become more concerned than greedy, buying power starts to dry up, and selling starts to gain momentum in reversing the uptrend.

Similarly, when the price moves down, buyers become fearful and try to sell at any available price, causing short sellers to become very greedy. Short sellers now become concerned about an overdone price decline. As short sellers become more concerned than greedy, selling power starts to dry up, and buying starts to gain momentum in reversing the downturn. Such strong emotional swings between fear and greed create a price trend in one direction until the market psychologically changes and the trend reverses. In order to define such trends, technicians draw their lines along these price swings, creating what they call trend lines leading to new expectations.

One may conclude, since such trends develop, why not make money by riding these trends up or down? And we'll be rich! That sounds like a joke, sure; this is easier said than done. Trends don't develop in straight lines; if they do, that would be possible and wonderful. This is how an ideal trend is. See Figure 2.1

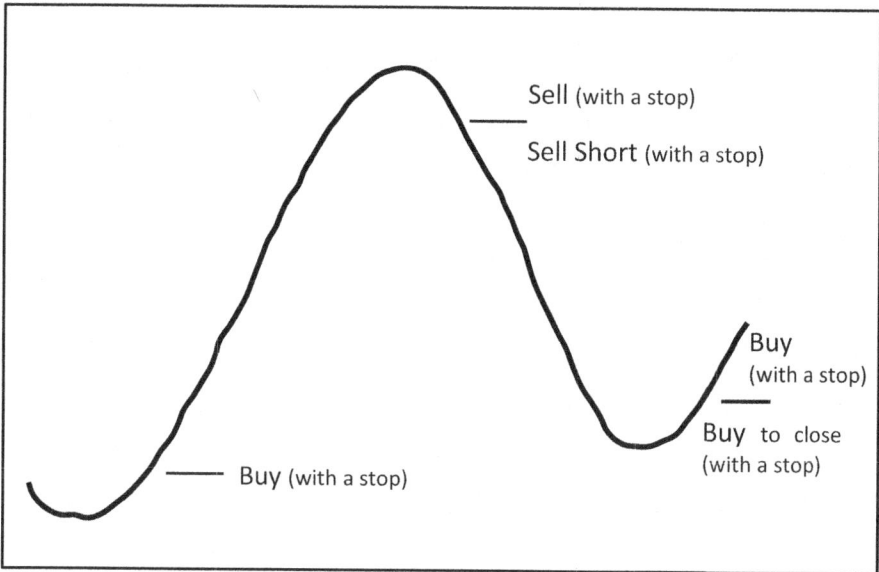

Figure 2.1 An Ideal trend

The market moves in a straight line in an uptrend and downtrend. The investor buys and holds until the uptrend reverses and hits the sell stop. Then, the investor sells short with a stop until the downtrend reverses and hits the buy stop to close.

We would ride such a trend all the way until it reverses, and then we ride it back in the opposite direction. It sounds easy, right? The only problem with that is the market never goes up or down in a straight line. Volatile moves and counter moves happen in both directions and throw everyone off. These are what we call "whipsaws" which make the life of every trader hell.

Whipsaws can drain your capital if you use stops, trying to limit your losses. And if you choose not to use stops, hope you will be lucky in guessing about the next trend. Simply, one cannot tell what would be the next move and whether the next move would be the start of a new trend or just another whipsaw. When we think the most logical next move should be in a particular direction, we often find the market moving in the opposite direction, wondering how such a thing can happen.

As usual, you would hear plenty of logical and not-so-logical explanations from professionals and not-so-professionals for every market move. I say that because many TV reporters start giving their views on the market when they are supposed to report just the financial news without injecting their opinions. The funny part is, they give the same explanation of whether the market moves up or down. How helpful is that? If logic and knowledge are the only things behind market moves, you would find all economists and highly educated people rich. There are plenty of smart people in the world who are willing to study every little detail about the market. The problem is the market has very smart and not very smart people. In fact, it's reasonable to assume that there are fewer very-smart people than not very-smart people. Each of these groups is pulling in different directions according to their opinions and understandings.

As a result of these variations in market participants, logic and knowledge are not going to influence the market one way or another without the great majority of market participants reasoning the same way. Thus, the market does what the market wants to do, reflecting the struggle between the market forces collectively.

Technicians realize that such unpredictable moves are very difficult to trade with just trend lines on the chart. They try to smooth such erratic moves with a variety of moving averages varying in time units and weight. Certainly, a moving average would smooth the chart when compared to the chart of the price. That may seem to be a good idea, nevertheless, it's not really that good. The problem with that is, we don't trade the average; we trade the price. The idea behind using a moving average is to yield a signal to initiate a trade once the price crosses the chart of a moving average in the same direction as the trend defined by the moving average line. Then one should hold that trade until the price crosses back the line of the moving average in the opposite direction. See Figure 2.2 Price and moving averages chart of the Dow for the Year 2022.

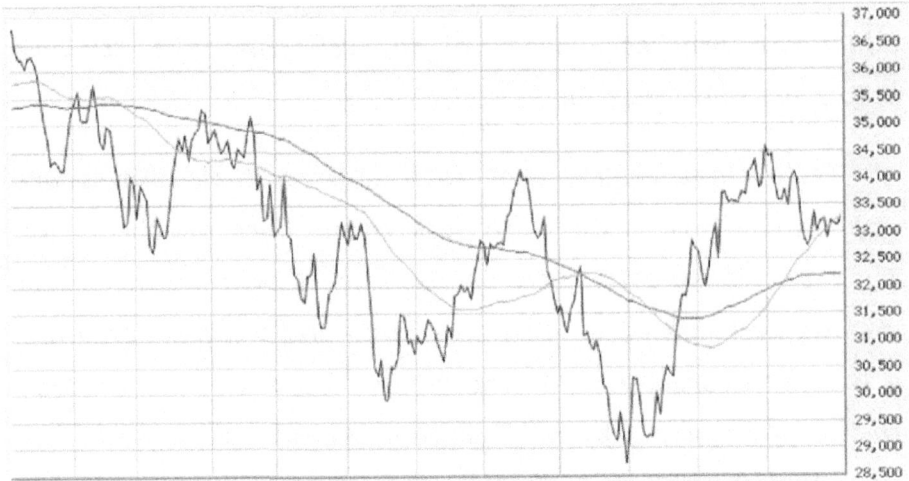

Figure 2.2 *price/moving averages (short and long) chart of Dow Year 2022*

That seems to be a good idea to eliminate most of the noisy fluctuations of the price if the trend continues for a long time. Unfortunately, that does not make our life any easier. Even in a fairly smooth market, the price jumps above and below the moving average all the time, triggering an action to initiate a trade. Following such a strategy yields many buy and sell signals, resulting in many whipsaws and considerable losses. Unless the price stays within the moving average for a long time, such a strategy consistently produces losses as the price swings back and forth above and below the moving average line. After all, we don't trade averages; we trade prices only.

If the price moves frequently above and under the moving average line, a trader would be buying at a higher price than what he sold initially or selling at a lower price than what he bought initially. Adding to these losses are the cost of trading, the commission on each trade, the spread between the asking and the bidding prices when a trade is executed, and the taxes on any capital gain from a few profitable trades.

To resolve this problem of triggering many buying or selling signals, technicians use a second moving average of shorter duration to smooth further the movements of price above and below the longer moving average line. That would certainly reduce the number of generated signals by price; only the signals generated by the shorter moving average above and under the longer moving average are considered. Nevertheless, while this strategy succeeds in reducing the number of trades, it fails to prevent losses. Using moving averages this way would always be lagging behind the price movements. The trader ends up buying at higher prices and selling at lower prices since the shorter moving average is much slower than the price movements.

Traders, as well as investors, might be tempted to think of their positions in the longer term to eliminate these whipsaws. For example, they may use a 200-day moving average instead of a 50 or 20-day moving average. They may as well use weekly or monthly data instead of hourly or daily data, with various moving averages applying the same process. Regardless of whether a longer or shorter term is used, minutes, hours, days, weeks, or months data are used, the process is always the same; only the number of trades is reduced depending on the number of generated signals for each trading term used.

Contrary to common belief, dealing with the market in the longer term is not any safer. The longer-term view is just a longer-term bet. The market may very well be way up or way down in the long term. Making bets on the outcome of the market is still gambling, regardless of which time frame is used. That certainly contradicts what most of us heard from professionals that the stock market has always gone up over a long time. The problem is how long is that long time? Most of these long-term studies use a hundred years in their research to conclude such results. That is very true when we talk in terms of a hundred years or more. If you bought the Dow in 1900, certainly by 2022, you made a fortune regardless of what happened during all these years. The problem with such thinking is we don't live hundreds of years to benefit from such studies.

Usually, our investing time in our lifetime is in the range of 30 to 50 years maximum. So if you get caught in a bear market for a decade or two, life would not be very pleasant. It would be worse if you bought at the peak of a bull market, and then experienced a bear market for a decade or more. You don't think that can happen? Let's see! In August 1921, the Dow was trading at 61, by September 1929, the Dow reached 381; it appreciated by 525% in 8 years. Most of us heard about the crash of 1929. The Dow declined from its peak of 381 to 41 by the Summer of 1932; it declined by 89%. If you were one of those buyers in September 1929, and you bought the Dow at 381, you would have waited until November 1954 to recover. It took 22 years to break even. See Figure 2.3 The crash of the Dow in 1929.

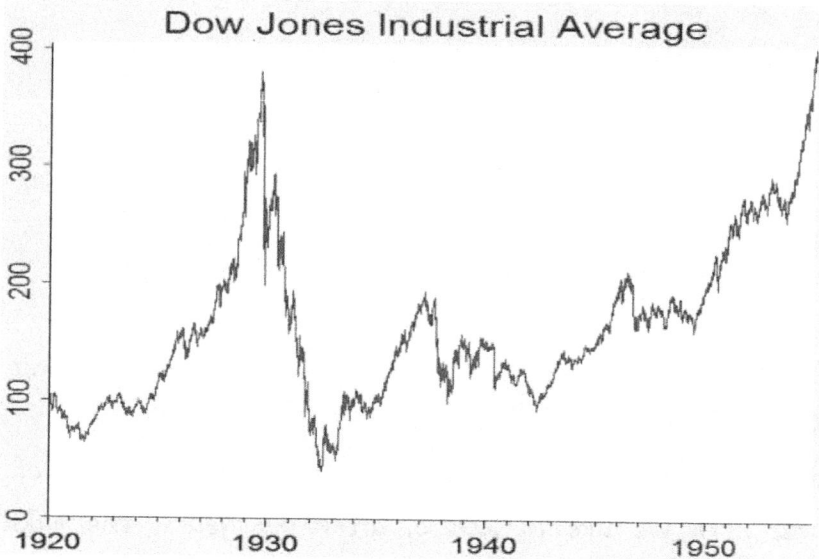

Figure 2.3 The crash of Dow in 1929

And for those who remember the tech bubble of 2000 when the Nasdaq was trading around 5000, and then it declined by late 2002 to around 1000; that's a decline of 80%! It took until 2015 to revisit its previous peak. Do you remember the hype of Dot.com? It seemed everyone wanted to jump on the internet wagon at that time. For those who bought at the peak of 2000, they had to wait until 2015 to recover with an inflated dollar after 15 years! See Figure 2.4 The crash of Nasdaq in 2000.

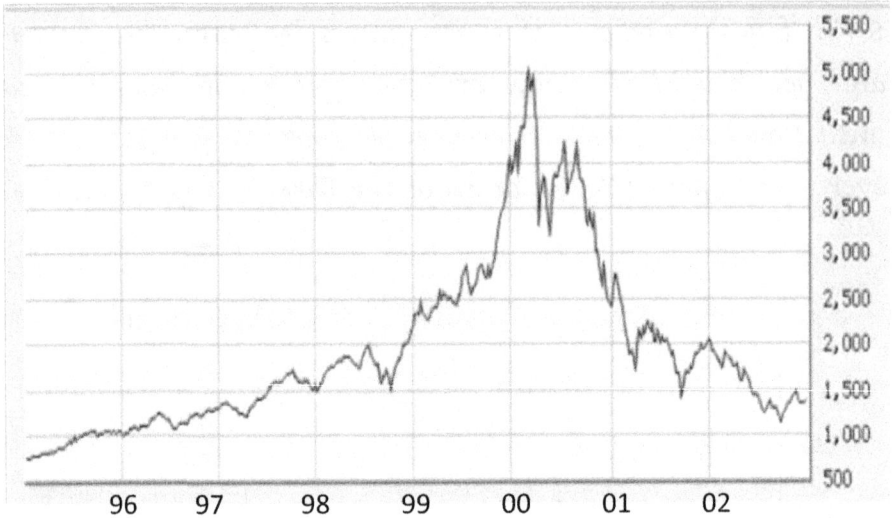

Figure 2.4 the crash of Nasdaq in 2000

Another example, Look at the Japanese market the Nikkei reached almost 40,000 in late 1989, then it declined until 2003 to about 7000; that's a decline of 82% and here we are in 2022, after 43 years, the Nikkei is trading at just around 28,000; it may never recover especially if we take into consideration the inflated currency. See Figure 2.5 of the Nikkei 225 from the early 1970s.

Figure 2.5 Nikkei 225

I think you got the point. How unpleasant your retirement would be if you have to wait for 10, 20, or more years to just recover your losses? What about if you're saving and investing for your children's college education, and you have to wait decades? That is the kind of misery nobody talks about when they talk about investing for the long term. For a middle age investor, that could be a disastrous time to wait decades to break even when there is not much time left.

CHAPTER 3

THE MARKET OUTSMARTS EVERYONE

We try to outsmart the market, but the market ends up outsmarting us. Regardless of how logical and knowledgeable you are, the market still can fool you. There are many conflicting forces in the market that you have no control over them, or to tell how these varieties of forces would react. Remember! Not all market participants think and react the same way as you do, and not everyone has the same logic and knowledge. So the outcome of the next move is impossible to predict correctly; that remains a guess. These millions of tiny, chaotic, and conflicting forces create an outcome that no one can foresee.

You might wonder why anyone with the right mind would stay in a declining market after a significant decline. Let me tell you this story about a frog which would answer this question. Suppose you drop a frog in boiling water, what do you think the frog would do? Most people might say the frog would immediately try to jump out of the boiling water if it can or would die struggling in a short time. I agree with that as well. However, if you put that frog in water at room temperature and then start to warm the water at a very slow rate, you might notice that the frog is not jumping immediately; it might not move much during the process. Of course, the frog would die at the end, but without that intense struggle.

In a fast-declining market, investors start jumping out of the market. But in a very gradual and slow decline, investors stay in the market hoping that the decline will reverse soon. Though the end result is the same, fast or slow-moving market, the losses become huge in the end. The way the frog dies, and the way investors lose their money, are not much different. When an event happens too fast, the reaction can be very strong and violent; but when the same event happens over a long time, there may not be much of a reaction. That is the scariest part of looking at the market in the long term.

Some readers may wonder why not use stop-loss in this case. Of course, I used stop-loss in the past; I don't use that anymore. These stops just eat gradually into your capital. A stop-loss might cut your losses short, but also it cuts your profit short too when the market swings back and forth regardless of where you put your stops. If you put your stop-loss far enough, your stop would get hit less frequently but with a greater loss. If you put tight stop-loss, your stop would be hit more frequently with less loss. Regardless of which way you're more comfortable, the end result is very much the same. Whipsaws will drain your capital along with fees and commissions. The only one who makes money is your broker, regardless if you make or lose money. The more you go in and out of the market, the more your broker makes money. That's why a stop-loss is very popular and extensively recommended by brokers.

Risking a small loss in order to have a large gain is certainly very logical, but that's easy to do only in an ideal market. An ideal market goes up in a straight line and goes down in a straight line without encountering whipsaws. Of course, a stop-loss is an ideal tool to use when the market reverses its trend. All you have to do is stay with the trend and use protective stops until the market reverses its direction. You collect your profit, and you reverse your position in the other direction. Isn't that wonderful?

Unfortunately, the market is anything but ideal, like everything in the real world. The market does not go up and down in a straight line. It moves in a very unpredictable way, fools everyone, and sucks back new money in it. Yes, the market outsmarts everyone sooner or later. When you think you are doing everything you learned about trading, and you hope to generate a profitable trade, the market makes its next move contrary to what you expected and your stop-loss is triggered, and you find yourself out of the market on the sideline with loss.

However, if you are unlucky, your stop-loss might be skipped and ignored in a fast-moving market when it gaps. While the market is way down and still declining fast, you feel the trouble you are in and the unbearable pain of loss, then you jump out of the market trying to avoid any further loss in a moment of panic. Imagine, after being kicked out of your trade, the market starts rebounding very fast as a strong wave of buying starts gaining momentum. Short sellers start buying to close their positions, and buyers who are on the sideline waiting for an opportunity start jumping in. This is a horrible situation as you sell at the bottom, and you miss the rebounding move, leaving you with your losses. Certainly, this is a very unpleasant feeling.

As you continue to use stops to protect your trades hoping to make a killing riding long trends, you would realize that the cost of this protection is more than what you can afford as it takes a large bite off your trading capital. Nevertheless, you should feel lucky if your stops are executed, even at limited losses. As I said earlier, often in a fast-moving market, stops are ignored. Only market orders are executed. If your stops are ignored, you would be looking at major losses. As you can see, whipsaws can be very detrimental to your capital. While the market might not be going anywhere but sideways, these whipsaws continue to generate more losses as the market keeps swinging back and forth, hitting your stops while you're trying to guess the right direction.

Would you call that investing or gambling? Is there really that much difference between guessing up or down a market, and guessing the head or tail of a coin, or the red or black on a roulette table? If you enjoy the thrill of guessing, then you most likely enjoy gambling. Consider the price you pay to be the cost of entertaining yourself. Certainly, this book will not be much of help to you. On the other hand, if you are like most people who are in the market to make money through investing, then this book can be of great help to you in dealing with the market.

One more thing to think about when trading in the market. Let's assume for the sake of argument that you are a super lucky trader unlike anyone else in this field. You often generate profitable trades with none of the problems I mentioned previously. Nevertheless, you still have a problem, not a small one. As a trader, you cannot put your entire capital in one trade, whether that is a stock, an option, a mutual fund, a commodity, or whatever. The risk is so great to use all your capital in one trade, regardless of how super lucky you are. Hence, as a prudent and wise trader or investor, you use a portion of your capital on one trade. That implies, you still have a sizable portion of your capital not invested. That by itself would bring down your overall investment performance. Money supposes to bring more money, not to sit idly doing nothing.

Some market participants blame their poor trading performance on the lack of time to be dedicated to the market. Dedicating a lot of time to the market would improve your connectivity to the market, but not your performance. Whether you sit in front of your computer charting your trades and monitor the market minute by minute or not, it's not going to make any difference. Many people think if they can follow the market instantaneously, they would be able to get in and out at the right time. That is easier said than done. When you look at the chart, you can easily tell where and when you should have initiated or terminated a trade. Sure, because that has been already done, and you see it on the left side of your chart.

Unfortunately, we trade only from the right side of the chart, where the next move is still in the unknown future. Many people think if they can monitor the market continuously, they would be able to avoid any trouble. Whatever time frame one uses in the market, human emotions and perceptions don't change. Fear and greed continue to be the strongest factor that leads us to act the way we act in the market. See if you can relate to this realistic performance chart in a downturn in Figure 3.1.

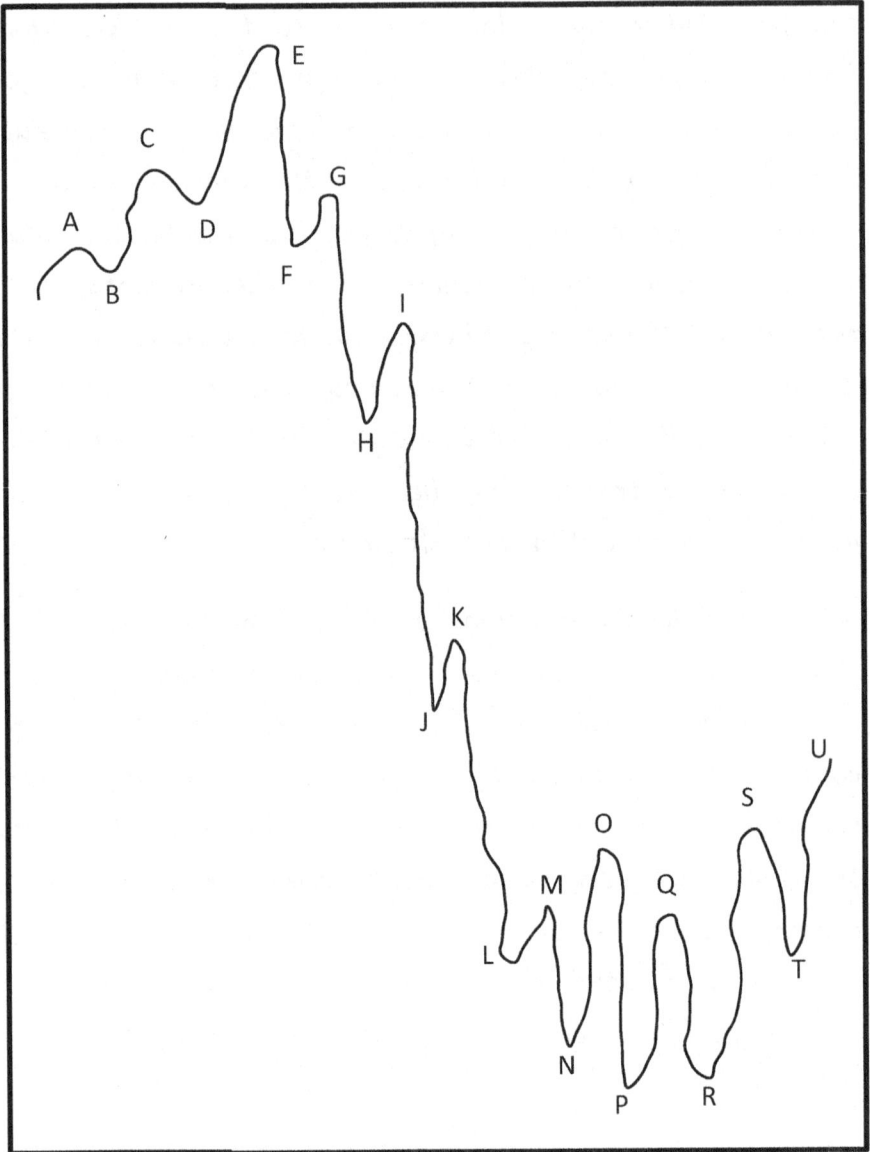

Figure 3.1 Realistic market in a downturn

Let's assume that we have a real-time quote service and see how one would respond as the market develops. I labeled every move on the chart for clarity in explaining those moves as they come from the right side gradually on the charts with their corresponding quotes. Try to imagine that every following point is not yet shown on the chart and see how most likely the trader's psychology is at each particular point.

- Point A: I see an uptrend is developing; so I am initiating a trade to ride this trend and let my profit run.

- Point B: Nothing to worry about, just a normal back step.

- Point C: That's what I thought, just a little back step. The uptrend is resuming now.

- Point D: Here it goes again, another back step. No one should expect the market to go up straight. I am used to that by now.

- Point E: Everything seems to be perfect, as expected. I cannot foresee anything that will change this powerful uptrend.

- Point F: Little correction to be expected. The uptrend will continue.

- Point G: I thought so. The market is now ready to take off again. I better take this opportunity to add more shares. I can use a stop-loss here, but I am watching the market minute by minute, no need for it.

- Point H: Wow! That was a fast decline with no apparent good reason, no need to panic, the market is sound.

- Point I: That was a steep correction. The market now has no other way to go but up.

- Point J: Oh God! What's going on? After all, it corrected already more than enough. I doubt it will go any lower after all this decline. I better start selling my shares on any good rally to recover.

- Point K: it's rallying, oh good! I should wait until I get back what I lost. Selling too early is a foolish thing to do.

- Point L: To hell with it! It's going down again. It does not look like it is going to stop declining. I lost most of my money, but I am not going to lose it all. I am selling all my shares now. I wish I sold earlier.

- Point M: It's bouncing back; I better jump on it before it takes off and loses my opportunity of getting back what I lost.

- Point N: I got whipsawed. I am not going to fall for such a trick again.

- Point O: Oh, I don't care, it's just another trick designed to suck back my money in the market. I will not buy it here.

- Point P: See? That's what I thought. It will go lower again. I better wait to buy at lower prices.

- Point Q: I am much wiser now and don't fall for these tricks. I will stand firm and wait for the price to drop lower, then I will buy.

- Point R: This time it must go lower. Let's wait a little more before buying.

- Point S: Ah! I can see something wonderful, a trading range. The next time it goes to that previous low, I will buy it.

- Point T: It is not supposed to stop here. It must go near the previous low of the range.

- Point U: I don't understand why it is taking off! There is no good reason to do so. It's taking off without me. I will wait for a correction before I buy.

I think you got the point! Do you feel the market has fooled you again and again with all the knowledge and arsenal you have? You are not alone. We all have our individual costly mistakes. You might have missed the right time to sell early enough before the decline. You ended up selling at much lower prices and lost most of what you gained or more. Similarly, you might have missed buying early enough to profit or at least to get back some of what you lost. Most likely you were whipsawed several times like most people. You could not see the downturn early enough. You did not see the trading early enough. Then you missed buying before the market took off again. Yes, all that was very hard to see before that actually happens. Now it's very easy to see it on the left side of your chart. That must be very frustrating to miss all these moves early enough when you have real-time quotes minute by minute, your computer charting and adding lines and indicators. Do you remember the story of the frog that dies regardless of whether you heat the water fast or slow? Do you remember the analog concept where things move slowly and gradually without being able to detect their motion until the move is already done? Maybe the lawn comes back to mind!

Looking back at the chart above gives the impression that trading such a market should not be really that hard. Yes, of course, but only if you are trading the market from the left side of the chart, as I said earlier. One may wonder why anyone would stay in an ugly downturn like that and end up with huge losses. However, when you trade from the right side of the chart as it's always the case in the real world, that easiness disappears. It's like driving with blindfolded eyes; you can see nothing! At every moment, you are facing again the same question: **which way is next?**

You might also think that traditional fundamental and technical analyses should have helped you better in identifying a trend ahead of time. However, your decisions and actions were clouded by your perception and emotions, swinging between greed and fear. Furthermore, in a fast-moving market, you will not get in or out where the lines cross on the chart. Besides, whipsaws can be real killers when you are trying to follow a trend. Stops might get you in or out early in a normal market environment, but you would be paying too many small losses which eat up some or all of the profit on some lucky trades. If you are a trader, you would realize how hard it is to time the market. Most likely, you would be lucky enough if you can perform better than the 75 to 85% of professional money managers who underperform in the market every year.

As for the buy-and-hold investor, who is betting on the direction of the market for the long term, he or she is in reality a long-term gambler, of course without knowing it most of the time. Since there is no way anyone can tell what would be the next move in the market, any betting on market direction in the short or the long term still has the gambling element in it.

So the question remains the same: Which way is the next move? Up? Down? Or sideways? The objective of this book is not to tell you which way is the next move. There are plenty of people out there who make all kinds of predictions. I quit doing that since long time ago. The wisest answer is to say "I don't know" and take it from there. People who try to predict the market are just imposing their views and opinions on the market. That is not the wisest thing to do.

The market is the last logical place on earth. Those who think they can reason their way in the market, demonstrate that they still don't understand well the nature of the market. All reasoning and analyzing go down the drain for a simple reason: Everything you know might be already known as well by other market participants. Therefore, all that is already reflected in the market and discounted. Even things that no one yet knows except you, assuming that is possible, cannot help you know the next move. Simply, you don't know how other market participants would act.

Imagine you're adding or removing one glass of water from the ocean. Such a tiny action has no impact on the ocean; it's irrelevant. A market is a huge place where many market forces are struggling against each other trying to create an impact to move the market one way or another. Only a powerful storm can create an impact on the ocean. Only a collective and powerful net force can move the market in a certain direction. The action of one or a few average investors would not make much of difference. Their knowledge and opinions are irrelevant as well when they try to predict the next move in the market. Remember, it takes a very powerful force in one direction to move the market.

People can pretend to have the ability to predict the next move. Some use fundamental analysis or technical analysis. Some even try to use artificial intelligence in predicting the market. Well, these people are highly technical and well-informed. Nevertheless, they are still playing a guessing game. Humans can be so arrogant, but the market demands its respect. When one imposes his opinion or views on the market, sooner or later, the market fools him, breaks him down, and kicks him out of this guessing game.

This is the wisdom on which the system described in this book is built. It's built on the assumption "I don't know" instead of the assumption "this way or that way" implying that "I know". By admitting that I don't know, I am giving the market its respect. I, no more, try to lead the market by imposing my opinion and predicting its direction. I simply follow the market. Likewise, I let the market tell me what to do. I would wait for the next move instead of trying to predict it. Can you see the difference? I know it sounds like a philosophical approach; it is in a way. The Buddha famously said, "life is suffering". That implies "living is difficult". This is a great truth! Once we realize that "life is difficult" everything seems to become easier. Why is that? As we anticipate difficulties, our attitudes change, our efforts increase to meet the challenge, and the difficult task becomes easier to achieve.

Similarly, there is wisdom when we admit "we don't know". We abandon our arrogance; we give the market its respect; we don't try to predict anything. We let the market tell us what the next move will be and what to do. You will smile when you hear someone on TV or in the elevator trying to explain the market and predict the next move. You would not need the opinion or the prediction of anyone. Unlike other systems that try to make predictions and give explanations and recommendations, this system, which I will describe shortly in this book, just follows the market. Now you can see why I say "I don't know". If you are an investor, this book would change the way you invest. However, if you tend to be a gambler-type investor, there are plenty of systems out there making predictions and many casinos as well to try your luck.

CHAPTER 4

UNDERSTANDING CYCLES AND ODDS

When we look at the beauty of nature, the mystery of the universe, and all the complexity of human life and other forms of life, we certainly have a lot to wonder about, appreciate, and discover. This book is about the financial market, but if your mind also wonders further in the spiritual dimension about God's existence, I do invite you to read my book "Does God Exist?" Read "The Proof". It's not a religious book, but a scientifically written book by an engineer, not a priest. A logical approach to the question of God's existence. Indeed, there are so many things to wonder about and be grateful for. All such amazing things have quite a bit in common. One of those common things is what we call the "cycle".

A cycle implies a repeated pattern or behavior which can be well-predicted with great accuracy. For example, the earth's rotational motion around itself results in one full turn every 24 hours. This repeated daily behavior of our planet earth can be called a cycle. The daytime and the nighttime are the two phases of this cycle. Note that these two phases of this cycle may or may not be equal at a certain time of the year. Similarly, one full turn of the earth around the sun is another cycle lasting 365 days or one year. To be more precise, this cycle is 365.25 days. For simplicity, we use 365 days, with one leap year of 366 days every 4 years.

A cycle can also be a sub-cycle of another bigger cycle, as is the case of a one-day sub-cycle relative to a one-year cycle. Our seasonal weather pattern also represents a cycle that keeps repeating itself in the same order: winter, spring, summer, and fall. This is a very predictable pattern. We usually don't question or try to predict their occurrence or the order they occur. They are so predictable to the point that we don't try to predict them anymore. They simply occur automatically and accurately, year after year.

Cycles are a far more normal occurrence to every form of life, other than planets' behaviors and weather changes. Look at your home garden, and you will notice all kinds of beautiful cycles in your flowers, plants, and trees. Cycles are not limited to nature and its physical components; they extend themselves to various aspects of our social, economical, and psychological life as well. For this reason, we would see a period of wars followed by a period of peace. Similarly, we would see periods of booms and recessions in our economy. Even our political and social lives experience this cyclical phenomenon through periodic shifts between our liberal and conservative views, opinions, and government as well. Such cyclical phenomena extend themselves into our inner-self as we experience periods of relative satisfaction and disappointment in our lives in general, in terms of careers, family, and relationships. The list is almost endless, but since this book is about investment, I will limit my discussion of this subject to only what concerns the investment world.

One particular cycle of special interest to all the people involved in the financial market is the business cycle. You can label it the "market cycle" or "economic cycle" since all these things are strongly related. This cycle has two phases as well, expansion and contraction if you're talking in terms of economy. During the expansion phase, business in general grows; during the contraction phase, the business usually declines. This business cycle and the relative change in the economy yield the market cycle.

When the economy is expanding and business is growing, companies are more profitable; therefore, stock prices rise. Alternatively, when the economy is contracting and business is slowing, companies become less profitable, causing stock prices to decline. These two phases of the market cycle are of special interest to investors. When all market conditions are moving toward a perfect mode, we experience the bull phase in the market cycle. On the other hand, when these conditions are getting less than perfect and deteriorating further, we experience the other phase of the market cycle, namely, the bear phase.

Such simplistic reasoning is certainly deceptive. Unlike the natural cycles in the physical world, which often can be accurately predicted, the market cycle is much less predictable. Figure 4.1 shows an example of an ideal cycle using a simple sinusoidal wave.

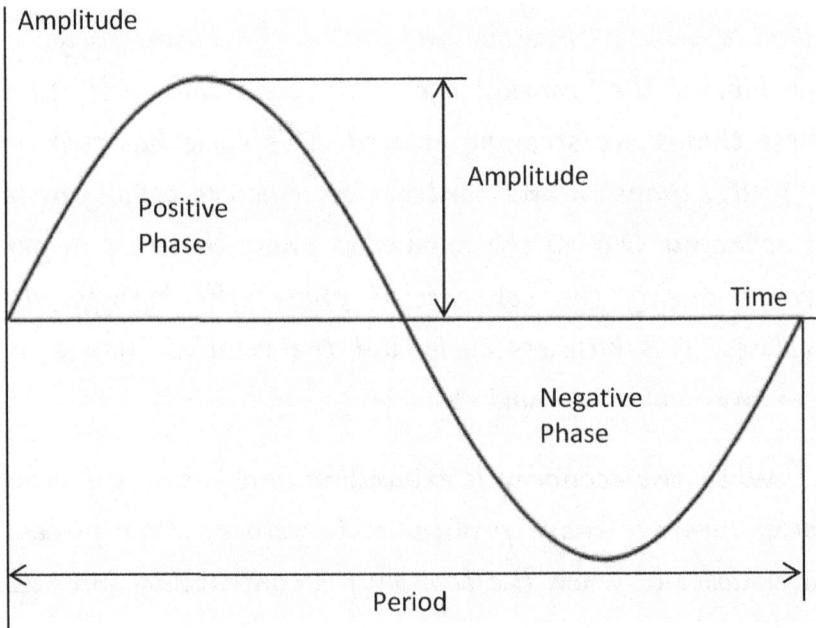

Figure 4.1 Ideal cycle

Note the time needed for the cycle to be completed from the start to the end. This is often referred to as the period or the wavelength. The amplitude is the rise or the decline from the neutral line to the peak or the bottom. In an ideal and repeated cycle, the period and the amplitude don't change. This ideal cycle has two phases, a positive phase, and a negative phase. Furthermore, the cycle spends an equal time in both phases and equal amplitude with a different direction.

There is an unlimited number of cycle forms that describe repeated behaviors of certain natural phenomena or man-made objects. Any cycle form, regardless of its complexity, can be very useful in predicting its changes as long as the cycle is likely to repeat itself in time and amplitude. In other words, if a particular event always changes the same way in terms of time and amplitude, such information can be very useful in many applications and very easy to predict as it repeats itself.

However, when we try to investigate the market cycle, we find ourselves playing a guessing game supported only by opinions, statistics, and luck. Although we know that every market cycle has a bull phase (rising phase) and a bear phase (declining phase) we still cannot predict the market moves at any time. The reason for that is simply the duration of the market cycle is always changing. In addition, the time the market spends during rising is different from the time spent during a decline. Furthermore, we don't know how much the market would rise in a bull phase, neither we can know how much it would decline in a bear phase. Not knowing the duration of the full cycle or the duration of its two phases, neither the rise nor the decline in amplitude makes it impossible for the market cycle to be predictable. In other words, we cannot determine the direction and the duration of the next market move. As you can see, investing becomes just a guessing game. When guessing is combined with betting money on a particular move, that is certainly another way of a socially accepted type of gambling called "investing".

Our inability to predict the next market move through cycle analysis leaves us seemingly with a game of odds. It's worth mentioning here that there are many people who try to identify market cycles in terms of days, weeks, months, years, and even decades. I definitely would not bet my hard-earned money on the accuracy of these cycles. Nevertheless, as confusing and unpredictable as market behaviors are, the market exhibits a very interesting trending ability that most participants try to catch all the time. This trending feature shows very often persisting behaviors that dispute any basis for the theory of a random market. Despite our inability to predict the next move, the market does what the market wants to do, but certainly not randomly.

Fortunately, the market has something most people hate, but it is of great interest to the system described in this book. That is, the market never goes up or down in a straight line. This fact may not be of particular use to most people, but it is very useful for our system, as it will be shown later.

Since my early childhood, I was fascinated with numbers and solving technical problems. I enjoyed studying mathematics, though I always wondered how much of that I could use practically in the real world. Later on, I majored in electronics and computer engineering. A particular area in mathematics was of special interest to me, statistics and probabilities. When I was a kid, I thought if one can figure out the odds of a game, then it would be possible to win in that game. Of course, that is far from true. Knowing the odds of a particular game yields a better understanding of the reward/risk ratio, more realistic expectations, and develop a better money management system in the game. In other words, just understanding the odds would not be enough to win, but that would produce a better-informed player. Forecasting the weather by knowing the odds of rain the next day would not give the forecaster any ability to change the weather of that day. The forecaster will be able to use that highly probable forecast to plan his daily activities accordingly.

This fascination with numbers and odds lead me first to Las Vegas, where I had an intimate relationship with its casinos. I was not the ideal type of player that casinos would like to welcome, a player who enjoys drinking and placing bets randomly. I was there for one reason, to beat the odds and satisfy my fascination with numbers, and of course to make money. Furthermore, I honestly, did not enjoy the environment of gambling. As I became more and more involved in the financial markets, my interest in the casinos faded away. My mathematical background and my understanding of the odds gave me better rewarding opportunities in the financial market. I was very surprised by how most casino players placed their bets. Either they did not understand the odds of the games, or being there and having fun was the main purpose of playing the game. After all, this is the price to pay the casinos to be entertained.

If we define a fair game as a 50% probability of winning or losing, we find, not surprisingly, that all games in the casinos cannot be defined as fair games. Of course, casinos are private companies and are in business to make money by entertaining people, but not for free. So letting casinos have a few percentages to their advantage seems to be a justified business practice in order to provide their customers with their gambling facilities. So let us take a closer look at the concept of a "fair" game, the justified small advantage the casinos have over their clients as the cost of doing business.

We defined a fair game as one that has a 50% probability of winning or losing. A simple example of a fair game is a genuine coin, which has two possible outcomes, a head, and a tail, that are equally probable to be the outcome when the coin is tossed up. Ideally, we should have the number of heads to be equal to the number of tails when the coin is tossed up. Realistically, however, one side of the coin may appear more than the other side, especially when the number of tosses is small. While the probability of one side to be the successful outcome is equal, that is one to two, nevertheless, it is possible to have, for example, several heads before the appearance of one tail, or vice versa. It is even possible to have nine or ten tails in a row before a head would show up. So what good the chance one to two would give us in predicting the next outcome of tossing up a coin? Practically, the answer is not much. At every toss, your chance of getting your desired side is the same, 50%. The reason is, every coin toss is an independent event. The coin simply does not remember if the last toss was a head or a tail. So for every new toss, the odds remain the same.

Unfortunately, many people have the tendency to resist such a conclusion. Since the possibility of getting a head or a tail is one in two, a gambler might conclude that sooner or later a head or a tail is going to catch up with the other side that did not appear in previous tosses. That is very true in one condition. That condition requires a very large number of coin tosses to bring the outcome of both sides of the coin very close to 50%. For example, if you toss up the coin 10 times, you might get seven heads to three tails or maybe more heads. Certainly, 70/30 is far off from the ideal odds of 50/50. However, if you increase the number of tosses to 100, you might get 60/40. And if you toss the coin 1000 times, you might have 550 heads to 450 tails, an odd of 55/45. Hence, as you keep increasing the number of tosses, the closer the odds get to 50/50, but it might never reach 50/50. For example, if you toss the coin one million times, you might get 506000 heads to 494000 tails, that's an odd 50.6/49.4, which is very close to 50/50. Although the odds keep getting closer to the ideal 50/50 as the number of tosses increases, the outcomes of heads to tails keep increasing too. In our last example of one million tosses, the difference between 506000 heads and 494000 is 12000 heads!!

You might be wondering why am I explaining such a simple concept when something like that is very common knowledge. In a casino, many "smart bets" are placed by individuals who think they have a powerful system that can beat the house. Such gamblers would try to double up, or maybe they developed a more sophisticated version of a doubling-up system. These individuals strongly believe that sooner or later, a head or tail will show up, and they will capture back all their previous losses plus one or two units in gain, depending on their system. They might apply their systems in any available game in the casino, whether it's Roulette, Craps, Blackjack, or even horse and sports events.

Let's continue our simple and fair game example with a coin. A doubling-up system may appear at first very logical and tempting for most novice gamblers. After all, a head or a tail most likely will appear after a few tosses, since the chance of having one side or another is one in two. Therefore, the system user may seem to be always winning after all. If that were true, you would not find one casino still in business in this world. On the contrary, casinos would love very much to welcome such "system players". Let's see why.

Most casino games have a minimum and a maximum bet displayed on their tables. These bet limits usually let you double up at most 7 or 8 times before you hit the table's maximum bet, regardless of the dollar amount used. For example, you might use a table with a minimum bet of $5 and a maximum bet of $500, or a table with a minimum bet of $10 and a maximum bet of $1000. See Table 4.1

Bet #	Min/Max $5/$500	Total Loss	Min/Max $10/$1000	Total Loss
1	$5	$5	$10	$10
2	$10	$15	$20	$30
3	$20	$35	$40	$70
4	$40	$75	$80	$150
5	$80	$155	$160	$310
6	$160	$315	$320	$630
7	$320	$635	$640	$1270
8	$640 (not allowed)		$1280 (not allowed)	

Table 4.1 A simple double-up system with different bets.

So the dollar amount of a bet is really irrelevant. Casinos impose such limits for a good reason. First, to protect themselves from big losses that players may win by luck. That also surprisingly protects gamblers from committing financial disasters by betting huge amounts of money. Imagine a gambler betting one million dollars just for the sake of recapturing all the previous losses plus one unit, say, for example, $5!!!!!!! That's insanity.

By limiting betting only between the minimum and the maximum bets, casinos deprive gamblers of the chance of recapturing their accumulated losses from earlier bets in doubling-up systems when they reach the table's maximum bet. While the purpose of the table's maximum bet is obvious, what's the purpose of the table's minimum bet? The minimum bet basically serves two purposes. First, the casino may not want to allow gamblers to entertain themselves by using pennies. Casinos, like all businesses, strive to reduce their business operating costs and maximize their profit. The 2nd reason for having a table's minimum bet is to prevent system players from expanding their doubling range from 7 or 8 bets to 12 or 13 bets. In a game of one in two outcomes, it is extremely unlikely to have 12 or 13 times in a row against the player. Certainly, casinos don't want to give gamblers such an advantage and reduce their revenues generated by higher bets.

You maybe are wondering why am I talking so much about gambling when the purpose of this book is investing. You might be like me, with no interest in gambling at all. Nevertheless, please bear with me for a little while, you will find out why this will be relevant to our investment objective in this book. As you can see in Table 4.1 shown above, Bet #8 exceeds the table's maximum bet regardless of any bet size in the different examples shown in the table. Therefore, Bet #8 would not be allowed.

Note also that any time you win before you reach the table's maximum bet, you would be capturing all your previous losses and winning only one unit bet, which is $5 on the 500-dollar table, or $10 on the 1000-dollar table. In other words, the next bet always equals the previous total losses plus gaining one additional unit. For the sake of a clear demonstration, I am using a simple double-up system in the table above. Of course, there are many variations and combinations of this system concept. Some of them are more or less aggressive than others. Nevertheless, all of them lead to the same disastrous results. That's why casinos would love so much to welcome such gamblers.

Why do such systems fail? Most people who use these systems fail to grasp the true meaning of these 50/50 odds in the real, practical world. Just because the chance of having a head or a tail in a coin toss is equal, that does not mean a head or a tail would alternate or appear an equal number of times, especially when a few coin tosses are considered. The tempting part to most gamblers is a head or a tail will appear soon enough, for example after 3 or 4 tosses and rarely after 5 or 6 tosses. Gamblers enjoy gaining one unit every time their desired outcome comes up and recover all their previous losses. That's wonderful, and everyone will be rich! Right?

Not so fast, the problem with this so called "system" is once in a while, a stubborn head or tail does not show up even on the 7th bet in a row. As shown in the above table, the losses will be huge at that level relative to all the previous gains. It would be much worse if that loss on Bet #7 happens at the beginning of the game without any previous gain. This is a disaster when that happens, and it happens from time to time. Imagine you're reaching Bet #7 on the 500-dollar table and you would be betting $320 to gain $5. If you lose, your total loss becomes $635. Similarly, on the 1000-dollar table, you would be betting $640 on Bet #7 to gain $10. If you lose, your total loss becomes $1270. This is a disaster! Chasing little money with a large amount of money always produces disastrous results and a painful experience. Casinos, certainly, have all the reasons to love such gamblers. Beautiful ladies will be waiting to serve these gamblers the free drinks.

So far, we discussed only a fair game, a coin. Forget about that! Casinos don't flip coins and don't provide fair games. They are in business to make money, not to entertain players for nothing. Someone must pay for those large, expensive casinos, and those free drinks served by those attractive ladies. For this reason, casinos usually have at least 5% or more of a built-in advantage in their games, with very few exceptions on certain bets of very few games. To say the least, they have no fair games at all. In fact, some of these advantages can reach as high as 25% on certain bets. After all, who pays for all that luxury in casinos? Who else except those players who go inside with pockets full of money and come outside with empty ones? You might agree as well as I do that casinos should have some advantage to stay in business.

Well, what does that advantage mean? So when casinos have 5% advantage, for example, how does that affect casinos and their players? That means one thing: For every

100 bets a player makes, casinos take in 5 bets. In other words, the longer players sit in casinos and make bets, the more bets they give away to these casinos until they lose their money. That is a guaranteed result for long-term gamblers. It's like hiding $100 under the mattress when inflation is 5%. With every passing year, the buying power of that $100 decreases by 5% or whatever the inflation rate is for that year. After several years, the $100 would have the buying power of just a few dollars.

While the purpose of hiding that $100 under the mattress is to protect it, nevertheless, that would eventually lead to the gradual loss of the value of the $100. So if you really want to gamble while protecting yourself against this long-term eroding advantage, it's best that you place all your gambling money in one bet. This way, the advantage the casinos have over you becomes much less. Otherwise, and like most gamblers, you would be paying for your entertainment. You are guaranteed in the long run to end up losing your money as well.

Does that mean no one can win in a casino? Of course not, some people win by placing a few large bets. If they are lucky, and they win, they should quit while smiling. But if a player insists on enjoying himself for a longer time, the chance of winning is almost zero, unless the player cheats or has a very good money management system. While I had long experience with casinos, honestly, I did not enjoy gambling or the casino environment. After getting heavily involved in the financial market, I lost all interest in casinos. The market is where the real money game is. Casinos are for gamblers who want to be entertained or novice players who still think that they can make fortunes by trying their luck.

But what if I tell you, for example, that I can let you have 16 bets instead of 7 bets for the same total loss shown earlier in Table 4.1 in a doubling-up system, what would you do? That might sound interesting because it's now much easier to win in a casino even with a simple doubling-up system. That is very true. So in a fair game like a coin, all you need is one head or one tail within 16 coin tosses to keep winning without costing you anything more than the loss of 7 original bets. It's extremely unlikely to have 16 heads or 16 tails in a row when the chances are one in two. This seems like a fantasy world! But what if I told you that I still don't like it, since I cannot stand the stress associated with gambling and any potential loss? What if I further told you that even if you exhaust all your 16 bets, you would not be out of the game? You would simply wait until the side of the coin you bet on appears. You might smile and feel tempted to try your luck, and you might start planning a trip to Las Vegas.

From our discussion of cycles and odds in this chapter, we can see that there is a strong relationship between the two subjects. Winning or losing in a coin game sometimes occurs in a series of one side only showing up. In financial terms, this is what we call a trend. Winning for a while, then losing for another while are basically the two phases of a game cycle as well. Unfortunately, this cycle cannot be predicted because the amplitude and the length of the cycle cannot be predicted ahead of time. However, understanding this cycle can be of enormous interest. If you can add a larger number of bets to our fair coin game example for the same amount of money, that would certainly improve our chances of winning. Furthermore, if you can wait for as long as it takes until the desired outcome shows up, the results will change dramatically to your advantage.

Having such a system can be a very powerful tool, not just an ideal thing to dream about or wish for. Such a system would become a money machine, not a gambling event or something over which you have no control. This is the kind of system I am writing about in this book. The same system I personally use and have been using for years only in the financial market. Notice that I said, "only in the financial market" and for a very good reason. Remember that I told you I hate gambling and I don't go to casinos anymore. You can treat the market as the largest casino in the world if you like gambling. Personally, I consider the financial market as the best place to make money.

While many people think that the financial market is nothing more than a gambling place, I do think the financial market is one of the best places to make money, certainly much better than casinos. How and why, you might ask?

Well think about it, dice on a craps table and a ball on a roulette wheel are not fair games, with big advantages to the casino side. Dice and balls have no memory, feelings, or sense of history. Ideally, there is nothing to prevent a roulette ball from landing on red instead of black many times in a row. Every new spin is a completely independent event, which has no relation whatsoever with previous spins. The odds are the same in every new spin for both red and black, regardless of previous spins. The ball simply does not remember where it landed previously, and neither it can feel your pain nor excitement. Certainly, such a ball does not count how many times it already landed on red or black.

On the contrary, the market does remember previous moves, which you can see on the left side of the chart. The market also feels market participants' emotions and knows where it has been. The market is the most emotional place on the face of the earth. Fear, greed, pain, and excitement are manifested openly and recorded historical data.

While the market cycle may not be a predictable cycle, it does exhibit very useful behaviors. Unlike most casino games, which behave randomly, the market does not move randomly. Every move the market makes reflects a considerable and continuous struggle between market forces. These forces are influenced by countless variables resulting from several social, economical, political, etc. factors. The market is a people game, not a coin, a ball, or a dice game.

That is why I prefer the financial market. People exhibit certain behaviors which sometimes reach extreme levels. These extreme levels of behaviors do repeat all the time because we are humans with typical behaviors. Human nature does not change as long as fear and greed are always a part of being human. These behaviors will continue to oscillate between these extreme levels, creating great market cycles.

CHAPTER 5

"TRADITIONAL" INVESTMENT: TRUE INVESTING OR JUST GAMBLING?

By now, we know investing traditionally using only fundamental and technical analyses does not add many advantages to the guessing game in the market. We also know that no one can predict the market, despite what many gurus out there claiming that within their abilities. Unless you are a gambler who likes to make a bet on the market, investing should not become another way of gambling in the biggest casino in the world, the market itself, when you really don't want to gamble.

The market game, I rather not call it a game, is also not a fair game when we have to consider fees, commissions, spread, and taxes you pay for your involvement in the market. Nevertheless, being involved in the market is a much more serious matter when compared to an entertaining game in a casino. Your hope for a better retirement depends on how the market would treat your retirement account. Your financial security and that of your family are at stake here and can become a major worry and concern every time the market makes large swings.

Should you buy and hold? Should you add to your existing position when the market seems to go higher and higher? Or you are more worried about the market valuation and considering selling? What about investing for the long term? Most professionals and financial advisers recommend that. Someone with great confidence might buy and forget about the market for many years, hoping the market will go his/her way. Certainly, you have many concerns about your future investments.

I heard someone recently saying that she does not invest in the stock market. She said that she invests only in mutual funds. As the discussion continued, I realized she did not mean that she just invests in mutual funds instead of individual stocks. She really thought that equity mutual funds are not a part of the stock market. I was truly surprised and shocked that this person did not know even that she was involved in the stock market through her employment with her company. It's really shocking and sad when someone does not even know that an equity mutual fund is an investment in the stock market. I guess the good thing is this person does not have to worry at all about the market since she does not think she is in it. I should admit this person has been very lucky during this long bull market. She unintentionally did very well as a buy-and-hold investor, much better than many market timers during this strong running bull market. Hopefully, she will become a better-informed investor before a strong bear market catches up and drains her retirement account.

You may or may not be surprised if I tell you that casinos don't gamble, even when they are in the gambling business. Neither do insurance companies gamble when they sell insurance policies. Casinos know that the odds are in their favor; they always end up winning in the long run. So do insurance companies too when they accept your policy bet on your car, health, home, or life. Casinos and insurance companies are in business to make money, not to gamble.

Similarly, we are in the market to make money, not to gamble when our intention is to invest. As I mentioned earlier in this book, there is a very blurry line between investing and gambling when we are involved in the market. Every time we make a decision to buy or sell a stock, a fund, an option, or a market, we are basically forming an opinion, making a prediction, and hoping that we will be right in the future about our desired outcome. But since the market is not a fair game with all the costs associated with investing, we might end up losing in the long term as well.

By now, if you are wondering whether traditional investing is just another accepted form of gambling, you are certainly close enough to the heart of my system in this book. Choosing a direction in investment is betting on a particular outcome, such as "up or down". Is it really that much different from a casino player betting on black or red in a Roulette game?

Does it really matter which gambling vehicle one uses? Betting whether the outcome will be up or down with such uncertainty when the chance of being wrong is as much or more than the chance of being right is just gambling in my opinion. Almost everyone in the market chooses a direction and bets on it. Isn't that precisely what gambling is? We pretend to be investing when we are actually gambling. Of course, in the end, some people are wrong and some are right. Do you call a lottery winner of millions of dollars a genius? People who are right at one time may not be as lucky the next time around. The "investing game" continues; winners and losers alike try to find a logical explanation for every outcome and move. Oh, the media is so good at showing their expertise, saying that sarcastically.

So what is investing for me? I certainly should not make you wait any longer for the answer to this question. Investing for me has no direction; whether it's up, down, or sideways, it's irrelevant to me. Whether I am right or wrong, it's irrelevant to me as well. Honestly, I don't know what the next market move will be, and neither do I care. You might be surprised or shocked to hear this unusual answer. Maybe you never expected to hear such a strange response. Yes, I said: I don't know nor do I care to know which direction the market will move. This answer may seem at first to be naive.

However, as you learn more about this system, you will see so much wisdom in this approach leading to a less traveled road.

Once you understand the true meaning of this approach, the difference between gambling and investing becomes very clear. Your worries and concerns when the market makes wild swings would disappear. You will never try to time the market again. Neither will you ever be just a buy-and-hold investor, betting your financial security just on your hope and opinion or other people's opinions that the market will go your way in the years ahead.

Remember! If you know what everyone else knows, then you know nothing that can help you see where the market will go. I look at the market as a business of buying and selling shares, not a gambling place. A business exists to make money and to provide some benefits to society. That is investing to me. Does it sound too ideal and philosophical? It might look this way at first. I admit this is a very unusual way of looking at the market. I don't predict the market direction; neither I do make a decision to buy or sell something based on my opinion or other people's opinions. You would be even more surprised if I tell you that, most of the time, I have no bias for the market to go up or down. Simply, I don't know what the market will do next. As I said earlier, I don't even care to know.

Of course I don't know what the market will do next, but why do I say that I don't even care to know? That must sound so foolish or at least so unusual way of looking at the market. Let us say for now it's an unusual way of looking at the market, and when you will learn more about the system in this book, you will be able to judge it best. Since I don't predict a market direction, neither I have a bias for it, I let the market do what the market wants to do. I just follow the market by buying and selling accordingly. My long and extensive experience in the market proved to me over and over that I cannot, neither anyone else can, predict what the market would do next except by luck. So why should I waste my time on a guessing game, when in fact I don't need to guess at all?

So instead of telling the market where it should go next by placing a bet based on my opinion and what I wish, I just follow the market and let the market tell me what to do next. I give the market its deserved respect. I don't impose my opinion on the market. When we make a bet on a market direction, we are attempting to outsmart the market by imposing our opinions on it. Yes, there is arrogance and foolishness when we disrespect the market. Can you see the wisdom of this approach? There is no need to impose our opinions on the market. Besides, betting in one direction is simply gambling. Predicting, guessing, injecting self-opinion, or listening to other people's opinions are just the best way in turning the market into the biggest casino in the world. Certainly, not the best way to turn the market into a profitable business. I treat the market as a business, not a casino. You will know more about the details of this system shortly.

Well, all that might sound great philosophically, but I am sure you are looking for a practical approach to investing. So, the question that might come to your mind now is how do I decide when to buy or sell if market direction is irrelevant? Let me answer this question by asking you a question. I know it's not the nicest way to answer a question by asking a question, but it's appropriate here. Which is more important, buying or selling? Does that sound like the chicken and egg argument? Does it really matter to know if the chicken or the egg came first? I guess not if you are not a chicken enthusiast. As long as more chickens keep coming out of eggs and chickens keep producing eggs, why not just keep eating chicken and eggs and stop our human nature from minding in the chicken business? Seriously, maybe you are not sure which is more important, buying or selling. My answer is neither one is more important; both of them are equally important. To sell something, you need to buy it first. Yet, to buy something, you need to sell something to produce enough cash, so you can buy what you want.

Let me ask you an easy question. Do you hate the price of something going down when you want to buy that thing? Of course not, you would love to buy it at a lower price as long as you believe it will go up again after buying it.

Similarly, you don't hate to see prices going up when you want to sell something, and you believe it might start going down soon. Do you see? It does not matter if the market goes up or down, as long as you buy and sell accordingly. Certainly, the buy-and-hold approach is not the best because we are imposing our opinions on the market by assuming the trend will continue to go higher. That's the gambling mentality again that comes with our human arrogance.

Whether it's a bull or a bear market, they are both needed to generate profit. In order to sell at a higher price, we must buy at a lower price. A bear market gained its ugly reputation because the public always bets on the upside direction. Besides, bear markets are associated often with troubling times in our economy and political systems. In good and booming times, people seem to be more satisfied and optimistic on average and are more willing to participate in a rising bull market. However, when a bear comes out of the bushes and the market turns south, the public hates it, especially when many people are fully invested. Therefore, the public can make money usually only in a rising bull market. Betting on the downside implies short selling, which is trickier for many people and considered an un-American thing to do.

Yet, people don't mind at all seeing a steep price decline in commodities such as crude oil, grains, meat, etc. Buying and selling simply create a balance between supply and demand, and both are equally needed. If commodity traders act the same way as the buy-and-hold stock investors do, we would see commodity prices going higher and higher, which is a recipe for disastrous inflation. The purpose of a bear market is to bring back balance to the market by bringing highly inflated prices down to earth created by people's greed during the bull phase. Both bull and bear markets are needed, in my opinion, to keep the market in balance. This balance in the market would prevent the excessive and overdone moves caused by excessive fear and greed.

This continuous struggle between the buying and the selling forces is what creates a marvelous, well-balanced free market system. Trading the two sides of the market is very healthy for the market system. Nothing of that should be labeled un-American. Without that struggle between these market forces, we may see, for example, the price of gas at the pump one day 50 cents, and the following day 50 dollars. These trading activities on both sides of a market keep prices in check and create enough liquidity in the market. As you can see, being unbiased to the market direction is the normal thing to do instead of playing a guessing game.

While most people hate a bear market, a bear market does not hurt. The lack of cash in a bear market hurts. The greatest money-making opportunities present themselves during a bear market, not in a bull market. You rarely can make any significant money after a long bull run. Great fortunes are made after a frightening bear run. If you live in California, as I do, you must be somewhat familiar with earthquakes. By now, you are either used to them or you are still terrified by them. In either case, you must hate them like everyone. Surprisingly, though, earthquakes rarely hurt; falling objects caused by these earthquakes do. Similarly, a bear market does not hurt, only the lack of cash during a bear market hurts. So you must be such a lucky person if it happens that you have a pile of cash during a nasty bear market. Believe me, it's definitely the opportunity of a lifetime.

Think of the financial market the same way as if you own a retail store business. I am sure you don't mind at all, seeing prices going down when you intend to buy your needed merchandise for your business and sell it later at higher prices. If you just buy and hold your merchandise all the time, how can you conduct your business and generate profit? Can you imagine going to your local neighborhood convenience store to find out that they buy and hold their merchandise and refuse to sell anything? That's precisely what buy-and-hold investors do. They buy stocks and hold them forever (well, a long time) expecting these stocks will continue to go higher forever. How can they be sure of such an outcome? Isn't this gambling? Stocks go up and down all the time; only a few of them are the exception. As a business, you would like to buy your merchandise at or below wholesale prices to sell them later on at higher retail prices. Buying and selling, as I said earlier, are equally needed to generate profit in your business.

Most likely you agree with this reasoning, buying wholesale and selling retail at a higher price. That sounds very much like what we are used to hearing all the time, "buy low and sell high". Yes, this is very true. Most people say and believe that. But again, most people end up buying high and selling low anyway. They do that unintentionally as they buy in a market trending up, then they sell when the market trends lower. Yet, some people (the buy-and-hold investors) usually don't want to sell at all!

Why does such a simple thing become so hard to do? Before answering this question, one might wonder what is high and what is low anyway? Something must be high or low relative to something, but relative to what? If a simple thing like "buy low and sell high" is so hard to do, it's because we don't know how high is high or too high, or how low is low or too low. Not being able to clearly define such quantities is the reason why such a simple thing becomes difficult to do, and often impractical and useless.

Financial advisers often shy away from trying to find out what is high and what is low. They simply advise people to buy and hold, assuming the financial market will resume its uptrend sooner or later. Many buy-and-hold investors assume that regardless of how high the market is at the present time, thinking the market will always go higher in the long run. Viewing the market this way implies anytime is a good time to invest. That might be a reasonable assumption in terms of many decades or a century, but that is not true in terms of the limited time we start investing until we stop. Though buy-and-hold investors don't think of themselves as gamblers, nevertheless, in my opinion, they are simply long-term gamblers, of course without knowing it. They do bet on one side of the market for a long time, assuming the market will go their way. While this might seem like "investing", nevertheless "betting" on market direction is another way of gambling.

Other people, however, feel uncomfortable with wild market swings, so they approach the market differently than the buy-and-hold investors. This kind of investor tries to time the market. Thus, they become market timers, or, in better terms, market forecasters. Nevertheless, all of them play the same guessing game. Some play the game for the short term; others play the game for the long term. Yet, all of them place their bets on the market and hope the market will go their way.

As shown, it's easy to say "buy low, sell high". However, it's not that easy when it comes to applying that in real-time investing. It's simply not practical, just to say the least. What might seem to be high, may go even higher; and what might seem low, may go even lower. Let's assume we want to buy low, as we are taught. Do we wait until the market drops 10%, or maybe 20%? But what if the market drops 50% or even 80%? If we buy when the market drops 20% for example, and the market ends up dropping 50% or 80%, that means we bought high instead of low. On the other hand, what if we wait for the market to drop 50%, but the market drops only 10%, then it resumes its advance? In this case, we definitely missed the whole thing. Gurus and market timers tell us that they are needed to tell us when to buy and sell. I admit, some individuals are far more experienced than the majority of other investors; nevertheless, many of these "experts" miss very often major moves in the market. Yet sometimes these experts predict the wrong direction altogether, underperforming the market and even the buy-and-hold investors type as well.

By now, if you have read this far in the book, you can see the problems with traditional investing. This is what inspired me to write this book to provide a new approach to investing. An approach that turns "investing" into true investing, or better words, a business-like approach to the market. This approach should provide a practical way to buy low and sell high without the need for guessing. Before I jump into the details of my investing system, I should establish the basis on which this system is designed to work successfully. So I must go through illustrations explaining why this system should not be used on some financial instruments.

Let us say, for example, that you like to invest in individual stocks. Probably, you might think that they can provide you with much better results than the overall market, as an experienced and savvy investor. Maybe you want to buy a stock of a company that you really like. The trend might be up, and the company has been profitable for a while. So you decide to buy that company on a dip, say, for example, 15%. The stock, unfortunately, keeps declining. Some shareholders think the company already reached its best, and maybe it's time to move on and head to the door.

However, since you like the company, and you do consider yourself a long-term investor, you would decide to keep holding it hoping it will come back soon. The stock, instead, sits there for a while, not doing much. After waiting for a long time, some shareholders lose patience and start selling again. The stock declines further and sits at the bottom. What do you do now? Would you sell it at a great loss? Would you add more shares since you liked the company to start with? Or do you just keep holding it, hoping it might recover one day? After all, you consider yourself a long-term investor, not a trader. Does that sound like a helpless situation?

Certainly, a stop could help you avoid the large decline. That is true in most cases, but stops can become very costly when a stock, or any other financial security, starts swinging back and forth. After all, how many times do your stops get hit, and you see shortly after that the stock reversing its direction? But let's assume you are a buy-and-hold investor; you would certainly have a problem on your hand now. The stock may stay there for a long time; it may go even lower. The general market might be going higher at the same time, while your particular stock is going nowhere. That is a very frustrating situation. Nevertheless, at least you still have the option of holding it with the hope that it may come back. But what if it does not come back? I am sure you agree with me that a stock can keep going higher and higher or lower and lower, or just sit there doing nothing for a long time.

When you bought the stock, the price trend on the chart and the earning report were appealing to you. But that was only the story of the past, up to the time you bought it. There was nothing that could tell you where the stock could end up in the future. In fact, many stocks, after reaching their peaks, never revisit these peaks again. Instead, they might keep declining for whatever reason to a few pennies and stop trading altogether. Nothing says that life cannot continue without that stock.

For this reason, I don't consider an individual stock an appropriate investment vehicle for my system. That would involve a lot of guessing and taking an unnecessary risk in addition to the inherited risk in the general market. That does not mean, I never buy an individual stock once in a while when I am in the mood to speculate and gamble. I am just saying that my system is not designed to be used on an individual stock as an investment instrument. As you can see from the example above, "buy low, sell high" is easier said than done. Many people may or may not realize how difficult to recover from an investment that has gone in a different direction. Let's crunch some numbers here, using a $100 stock as a sample to illustrate and understand percentages.

Table 5.1 Understanding percentages

Stock Price	% decline in price	% needed to break even
$100	0%	0%
$90	10%	11%
$80	20%	25%
$70	30%	43%
$60	40%	67%
$50	50%	100%
$40	60%	150%
$30	70%	233%
$20	80%	400%
$10	90%	900%
$5	95%	1900%
$4	96%	2400%
$3	97%	3233%
$2	98%	4900%
$1	99%	9900%
...	...	...

Notice the table is not finished yet! A stock can decline further. If the $100 stock declines to one dollar, your loss is now 99%. Some people think they need 99% to recover, not true! They need 9900%!! It's almost impossible to recover at that point. Some stocks go to pennies. In this case, it's most likely the company is bankrupt, and its stock is going to stop trading. My point is, if you lose such an investment, it would be impossible to regain what you lost.

From the table above, we can see how difficult to tell how low is too low, and how high is too high. High and low are something relative. Theoretically, there is no limit to how high a stock can go up. Similarly, we may think once a stock loses a big chunk of its value, our risk may seem to be very limited since a stock cannot go lower than zero. Not true! Think about it! Suppose the above $100 stock declines to one dollar. That would be a decline of 99%, you still can lose 50% if you buy that stock at one dollar, then the stock declines later on to 50 cents. As you can see, even with a decline of 99%, you still can lose an enormous amount of your investment.

Most people think that the upside is unlimited, but the downside is limited to zero. That is true if you buy the stock at $100 and the stock goes down to one dollar. At this point, you would care less if the stock goes to 50 cents, for example. It becomes irrelevant at this price. However, if you buy the same stock at one dollar thinking you had a great deal, think again! If the stock drops only to 50 cents, you would lose 50% of your investment immediately.

My point is, regardless of how low a stock goes, it may not be too low or low enough to eliminate risk. This risk is always there. In fact, a stock that goes that low becomes much riskier. It's more than likely it would go to zero, and you would lose 100% of your original investment, regardless at which price you bought it. As shown above, an individual stock has a built-in risk, regardless of how far up or down its price moves. A company simply may continue to grow or may go out of business and its stock would disappear.

Well, since an individual stock does not seem to be a suitable investment, you might be wondering if a mutual fund is. A mutual fund, as we know, is a basket of many stocks. Many mutual funds have more than a hundred stocks. One might think such a fund is less likely to go to zero. That is true, however, I will never invest in an actively managed fund. While some funds come with loads, all mutual funds have additional fees of about 2% to operate their business. Furthermore, mutual funds distribute capital gain even to shareholders who may not even have any gain. Even worse, you might see some capital gain to be taxed even when you have losses on the fund shares you own. How unfair is that? That happens when a fund starts selling some profitable stocks before new investors buy the fund. The new investors become tax liable on all capital gains distributed by the fund, regardless of whether the new investors realize any profit or loss.

Furthermore, when you own a mutual fund, you are a sitting duck in a fast-moving market during trading hours. The market might have a huge drop or an enormous rally during the day for whatever reason. Mutual funds investors cannot take advantage of these wild moves at the time of their occurrence during the trading hours. That happens because when you buy a mutual fund, you are not buying directly the shares of the stocks owned by the fund. You are buying, instead, the shares of the fund itself at the net asset value price.

Mutual funds' net asset values are computed daily using the closing prices of their stocks at the end of the trading day, regardless of what happened during the trading hours. In other words, the market might crash or jump during trading hours, then it might end up unchanged. Mutual funds investors cannot act on that at the time of such big moves. Your transactions would be affected only by the closing price, regardless of when you call your broker to make a transaction in your mutual fund. You would be paying the price of the computed net asset value at the close price at the end of the trading day.

Nevertheless, the disadvantages stated above are not the only reasons why I don't like to use actively managed funds in my system. Statistics show consistently about 75 to 85%

of these actively managed funds underperform the market year after year. Of that 15 to 25% that outperform the market in a particular year, most likely and most of them underperform the following year. You can check the performance of most funds against that particular category of the market. For example, you can check an energy fund with an energy index, etc.

Like most people, fund managers are humans too; that is, they become fearful and greedy too. While they are clever, highly educated, and experienced individuals, they still often underperform the market. Actively managed funds invest for the long term. They start to buy or sell stocks after big moves, say 20% or more. One cannot expect a fund that manages billions of dollars to dump its stocks just because the market drops 5 or 10%. Most funds don't even bodge before a drop of 20%. Some don't react at all; they just ride the move. Worse than that, some of them sell only after a large drop when they become convinced enough that the bull market is over. That may happen when the market is bottoming and when the pain becomes unbearable. Similarly, they don't buy back until they are convinced enough that the bear market is over after a large move up by the market. They simply miss the opportunity to make up what they lost. In other words, they get whipsawed like everyone else, with an additional disadvantage. They are less flexible than individual investors. As an individual investor, you can just get out of a bad position with a click of a mouse or a phone call.

It's much harder for a fund to dump billions of dollars worth of stocks very fast. If the market's next move proves to be a false move, that is, the trend resumes instead of reversing, these funds would get whipsawed twice. Their losses become enormous, far more than the market's losses. That's why they cannot be as flexible and cannot react fast enough.

Another thing I must mention, regardless of how sincere, committed, and hardworking these managers are, their pain is relative while the investor's pain is real. What do I mean by that? I say that because their performance is compared to other funds' performance and to the market's performance as well. So if the great majority of funds are down, say by 35%, and the market is down by 30%, but your fund is down only by 25%. In this case, your fund manager would feel great and may celebrate that as well. Fund performance is compared to other funds of the same categories and also to the market.

To illustrate that better, imagine a teacher who grades on the curve. So let's say all students do poorly in the class, but some students do less poorly than others. The students who do less poorly end up with an "A" grade regardless of their true knowledge, since they are the best within the worst on the curve. They are simply graded because they are "better" than their peers, not because they are really knowledgeable. While your fund manager is celebrating the loss of only 25% compared to the 30% loss of the market and 35% loss of the other funds, you would be out of 25% of your real money. Should you celebrate too because you lost less than the rest?! That's why I said earlier that your pain is real; your fund manager's pain is relative.

After a long deep decline in the market, shareholders cannot bear their pain anymore whether their fund manager is outperforming the market or not. Pressured by the shareholders redeeming their shares, the fund comes under pressure to dump more shares to generate enough fund to meet shareholders' redemption demands. Like most people, these fund managers don't buy any shares until they become very convinced that the market has reversed its direction. By the time these managers become convinced that the bear market is over, and a new bull market is in the making, they miss a great deal of the recovery movement in the market.

Most fund managers, in this case, simply drop their losing stocks at very low prices and buy the popular hot stocks at considerably higher prices. This change in portfolios is what we call "end-of-quarter dressing" which happens all the time when fund managers update their portfolios to make them look more attractive on their quarterly statement or prospectus. The great majority of these actively managed funds get in and out of their stocks very late, understandably funds cannot be as flexible. Therefore, they continue to underperform the market.

While all the reasons stated above are mostly a general concern for investors, the real reason why I don't like to apply my system on actively managed funds is that my system works so much better on "raw funds" that mimic exactly what the market does. As I have shown above, an actively managed fund is basically involved in doing some trading. Since its lack of flexibility and its efforts to avoid the market's whipsaws, often it sells shares late at lower prices and buys shares late too at higher prices, causing the fund to underperform the market.

For this reason, I strongly lean toward a fund that does not do any trading, a fund that just mimics the market as much as possible. For now, the main point is, I want to preserve those large swings in the market. This market volatility is very profitable to my system. You might be surprised, but the more volatile the market is, the better performance my system yields. Actively managed funds distort the market's moves through their trading and market timing, since their objective is to outperform the market. That is perfectly fine for most mutual fund investors. Nevertheless, this book is not about mutual funds investing. It's about a particular and unique system and a new approach to investing. In fact, all the system needs is a fund that just mimics the market without any distortion.

CHAPTER 6

THE COMMODITY CONCEPT

As we continue to explore other types of investments that can be applied to the system, we will examine other investment possibilities. We saw that an individual stock can go to zero and possibly stops trading altogether. While a mutual fund's net asset value share does not go to zero as easily since it is a basket of individual stocks, we saw that actively managed funds are not suitable investments for the system discussed in this book for all the reasons I mentioned in the previous chapter.

There are other types of funds that are worth mentioning, the "funds of funds". This kind of fund invests in other funds instead of investing directly in individual stocks. The portfolios of such funds consist of other stock funds, bond funds, and other securities. In other words, instead of having one store, you now have a large mall with many stores in it. While this type of fund is well diversified, its unusual composition of a wide range of securities does make it much less flexible without the ability to mimic the market moves. Certainly, it's not the type of security I would apply to my system.

I should add some cautious words regarding all these types of funds, especially the actively managed funds. Often, when the net asset share price of a fund becomes so low, the fund simply decides to reverse split the share price by a factor that brings back the price in line with a more normal range. This is a marketing strategy used widely by funds. Investors who are not aware of this practice can be misled, thinking that everything is fine with the fund or the stock. Usually, this process takes place when a company or a fund increases the price of the share of its stock or the share of its fund and reduces the number of its shares, perfectly legal and common practice to improve the marketability of its securities. The fund then seeks fresh money from new investors through marketing and advertisement and continues business as usual. Definitely, this is not something I can apply to my system.

Well, what about options? Options are volatile enough, so can they be used? They are very popular and too much hype is made about them. The answer, however, is also NO. The objective of the system described in this book is to manage a whole portfolio, not to get stuck in individual trades. No prudent enough investor would make options the only assets of a portfolio. Options are very well known to be "wasted assets". When these options have no intrinsic value, time premium becomes the only thing that contributes to their values. Therefore, when their time runs out, options become worthless.

Nevertheless, options are extremely useful for traders and speculators. They can be used simply as "lottery tickets" to speculate on the underlying securities, as most people use them. They can also be used as hedging tools or other combinations by professional traders. While options cannot be used as the main instrument for my system, they can be used to generate income by writing covered options for buying and selling shares. I will revisit this subject later on in discussing the details of the system, as one optional tool, but not required.

There are several strategies that use options, which can be illustrated in many options books that you can find in many bookstores. Such strategy details are beyond the scope of this book and are irrelevant to the system described in this book. However, it might be of some interest to us to consider the odds and the possibilities of generating profit in the options world. Let us assume for a moment that the odds of guessing the direction of a particular financial security (a stock, an index, a commodity, etc.) are as that of a fair game 50/50. So your chance to be correct in your guessing the direction of the underlying security is one to two. Nevertheless, such an assumption is incorrect when it comes to options. We know that financial security can go up, down, and sideways. Until now, we ignored the third outcome, namely the sideways. If you hold only the security by itself, the sideways outcome is irrelevant in the short term because you can hold a stock for an unlimited time as long as it exists.

However, when dealing with options, time becomes enormously important. If your option does not go "in the money", by its expiration date, that option becomes worthless. Therefore, the sideways outcome becomes very relevant as the other two outcomes, up and down. So now we have three possible outcomes with odds of 33.3% instead of two outcomes with 50% odds. Your chances now to be correct in guessing the outcome of the underlying security for an option play would be one to three.

For example, if you buy an at-the-money call option on a particular stock to go up, the premium you pay for that option would be entirely time premium. The option has little or no intrinsic value, depending on where the stock price is relative to the strike price of your option. So if the underlying stock goes down or moves sideways, you would lose 100% of your initial investment as your option expires worthless. Even if the stock goes up slightly, you may still lose a good portion of your option premium, since the intrinsic value of the option may be less than the total premium you paid initially.

So in order to make a profit on your option, you need the underlying stock to move fast and strongly upward to overcome the decay of the time premium and also to reach an intrinsic value greater than the premium you paid. As you can see, your 33.3% would be even more reduced to about 20% at most. Your chance now of losing this trade is 80%, and that's for an option at-the-money. However, if you buy an out-of-the-money option, all I say is good luck. Your chances are now almost certain that you would lose your premium option unless your underlying stock makes a huge move up immediately, which is very unlikely.

Of course, once in a while, your option goes in-the-money and you would make some money on the premium you paid for the option. As I said earlier, options are just lottery tickets and wasted assets. You might have a better chance of making a profit on your bet in a casino game. At least you can have about 45% chance of winning instead of just 20% or less. At least you will be more entertained in the casino. So when you hear someone claiming that he or she doubled or tripled their option premiums in a few days or weeks, remember all the past losses that they don't mention. Also remember the premiums paid for options are very small amounts of money. Doubling a few hundreds dollars is not the same as doubling a whole portfolio of 100 thousands of dollars.

After all, only the overall portfolio performance should be counted at the end, not just few tiny lucky shots.

Doubling your premium option once in a while, but losing your option premiums most of the time, is not something to brag about. The great majority of options traders end up being on the losing side. So much for the "limited risk and unlimited profit" sale pitch we always hear. Frankly, I don't see how risk is "limited" when one loses his entire original investment. For those who don't know how to trade options properly, options take them nowhere except to the cleaner.

Nevertheless, for those people who like to gamble, options are another way to gamble as well. Now, in fairness to options trading, some strategies can be well incorporated with the underlying security and make a lot of sense with very little risk. I will talk about that later on as I introduce the details of my system in this book. That approach will be optional only; it's not really necessary in the application of the system.

Well, what else is left to consider as a useful investment instrument for my system? I am coming up with the answer very soon, but it's important to know what to not use with the system described in this book. But do you still remember our fair game discussion in chapter 4? As we saw in that chapter, when you reach the 7th bet in Table 4.1, you would be in big trouble and out of the game. Luckily, the financial market, except for the options, gives you the ability to stay as long as you want to hold your stock or your fund hoping that they may come back after a decline.

Now you don't have to be kicked out of the game anymore. Instead, you can wait for a possible recovery. That is a considerable improvement on a casino game! If you can wait in a casino game until your desired outcome shows up, you would not find an empty chair in the casino from the crowd. You simply can do that in the financial market at any time. This is a built-in advantage. I also said previously, that a stock may or may not come back. Similarly, an actively managed fund may keep losing its share value even while the market is going up.

You basically need something that never goes to zero. Something would not be affected by whipsaws and additional costs like actively managed funds. This is when my system becomes very effective and very needed in the financial market environment. But what else we can use that can be suitable for the system? We already discussed individual stocks, actively managed funds, and options. Bonds and bond funds are not good instruments for this system either.

Let's examine another type of investment that would not possibly go to zero. How about commodities? Physical commodities don't ever go to zero as long as people and animals need to eat. People would always need to consume energy and build things from raw materials. You can bet that the Dow Jones would go to zero before corn or wheat reach a zero value. If the unthinkable happens and our western civilization and free market system come to an end as a result of a great war or an economic and social revolution, the Dow may or may not go to zero. Early in the 20th century, communism did away with many free market systems in several countries. Certainly, communism failed miserably economically by the end of the century and collapsed. Nevertheless, even with such a slim possibility for the stock market to go to zero, the possibility for the Dow to go to zero is greater than that of corn and wheat. Simply, as long as life exists, people and animals need to eat to live these foods, regardless of whether they have a free market system or not.

Commodities are the ideal investment vehicles. They always come back and always fluctuate. They never keep going up, or they never go to zero or out of existence. It's very American to buy them and sell them short, too. People would love to pay less for their food and energy. Only farmers and oil companies hate to see lower prices. Commodities always move up and down unlike stocks, which may keep moving in one direction for a long time, and in some cases, they simply disappear.

Unlike stocks, commodities prices move up and down in a relatively defined range. This range is adjusted in time by inflation and the variations of the dollar. We don't expect commodities prices to keep going higher and higher or lower and lower, like stocks. Therefore, commodities exhibit some cyclical characteristics, not well-defined and accurate cycles in the ideal term. Nevertheless, these price movements fluctuate clearly and repeatedly between peaks and bottoms with time. Of course, we cannot tell accurately the amplitude, the phase, and the length of the cycle, but we can see clearly these repeated fluctuations which are something that cannot be seen in individual stocks. These cyclical characteristics of these physical commodities happen unless some unnatural forces like OPEC in the case of crude oil, corn government subsidies, central banks manipulation of gold, etc.

In relatively normal economical and agricultural conditions, corn, for example, fluctuates between $2.50 and 6 or $7 per bushel. It's almost impossible to imagine that corn in normal conditions would trade at $100 a bushel just because investors bid the price of corn, as they do with some popular high-tech stocks. The reason for such cyclical movements is the natural law of supply and demand. When corn becomes so cheap, say for example $2.50 with no government subsidies, corn would be selling near or below its production cost. Like most people, farmers don't like to work for free, or worse, work at a loss. Therefore, they reduce or stop planting corn and switch to planting another product, wheat, for example.

This reduction in the supply of corn combined with the high demand caused by the low price would create the condition for higher prices of corn. This is what prevents corn from going to zero. At higher prices, corn becomes more profitable, so farmers rush to plant so much of it. The high price would cause supply to increase, but that would also decrease the demand for corn, preventing the price of corn from further unreasonable higher prices. This cycle keeps repeating itself time after time unless severe weather conditions and/or monetary interference by the government exaggerate the move one way or another.

In this case, we might wonder why doesn't everyone trade commodities if they are more predictable. One of the main reasons that not everyone trades commodities is the extremely high leverage involved in trading them. When you buy an individual stock or a stock fund, you pay 100% of the share price with no leverage. If you are a more aggressive investor, you may buy them at a 50% margin. Therefore, you would be paying 50% of the price and the other 50% would be borrowed money. If your stock moves up 50%, you would make 100% of your initial money. However, if your stock moves down 50%, you would lose 100% of your money (the 50% you invested initially and the 50% you borrowed to invest).

This process is similar to trading commodities, except with much higher leverage. Most commodities allow you to trade them with only 5 to 10% of the commodity's total value! As a result of such high leverage, a small movement in the commodity itself would create a magnified impact on your initial investment, up or down. This is why profit and loss are magnified in commodities trading. For this reason, commodities trading is best left to professional traders and speculators. That's why most people usually keep commodities out of their portfolios.

Ideally, commodities should be the perfect investment for my system, since they always come back sooner or later. Practically, however, they are not the best investment, as well. The reason is, when you trade commodities, you trade them in the futures market. As the name implies, they are traded in the future. If you think a particular commodity is going up in price, you may initiate a long position by buying a futures contract for a particular month. This month of delivery of the underlying commodity can be a few or several months or even years in the future. So you will be speculating for example on corn 9 months from the present or even years. You can also buy commodities in the spot market by paying for the underlying commodity and taking delivery. Unless you are a large manufacturer of cereal, for example, no one would buy corn or wheat as an individual investor. That's why commodities are used by traders just as speculation instruments in the futures market. Only manufacturers take delivery of the physical commodity at the expiration of the delivery month. So you certainly don't want 1000 barrels of crude oil or 5000 bushels of corn dumped in your front yard.

The delivery month in the far future is usually much less sensitive to the spot price and much less volatile. Similarly, if you think a particular commodity is going down, you might want to initiate a short position by selling short that commodity. While the spot price is ideal for my system, the future price is not at all. The spot price of the commodity reflects what is happening in the present, however, the future price might be little affected or not at all.

One more thing I would like to talk about regarding commodities. In recent years, a new family of funds came into existence, the Exchange-Traded funds (ETFs). What are they? They are funds, as the name implies. However, these funds are traded on the exchanges like individual stocks at any time during the trading hours of the exchanges. This is definitely a great advantage over mutual funds which their share values are computed using the closing price of the trading day in their net asset value.

These ETFs are used to trade many financial instruments during trading hours unlike regular mutual funds. Some of these ETFs are used to trade the general market indices such as the Dow Jones Industrial Average, the SP500, the Nasdaq, etc. ETFs are also used to trade sector indices, such as high-tech, energy, and healthcare, etc. You name it, and you will find an ETF for it. ETFs are even used for trading international markets and commodities as well. So now if you don't want to trade an individual technology stock, for example, you can simply trade a technology ETF as an individual stock during market hours.

The technology ETF is composed of several technology stocks, which adds diversification and convenience.

While ETFs are a great way to trade any group of financial securities, they do have some awful disadvantages. These disadvantages are very detrimental to your financial health. If nothing jumps at you in this book and rewards your time and effort in reading it, just understanding this side of ETFs can save you thousands of dollars being lost in dealing with the market. Let me explain what I am talking about.

Many of these ETFs, including commodity ETFs, end up consuming gradually a great portion of your investment. I would not be exaggerating if I describe that as a rip-off. For example, you see corn trading at $2.50 a bushel. This is a great price, and you think it's a good time to trade corn. But you don't want to deal with the complications and the hassles of trading the commodity itself in the futures market. You would realize that you can trade corn in an ETF like an individual stock on the exchange without the huge leverage required in trading the commodity as I explained previously, isn't that wonderful?

So at $2.50 the price of a bushel of corn, let's assume your ETF's share price is $10. Great, you decide to buy 100 or 1000 shares of that ETF corn when the corn commodity is trading at $2.50/bushel. Then you wait for the price of this commodity to increase, say for example, to $6 or $7 per bushel.

Now you might need to wait some time for the corn to increase in price, maybe months or a year or two. Meanwhile, the way the ETF's share value is computed daily would be draining very gradually your initial investment. By the time, corn moves to 7 dollars, for example, your ETF's share value should be much more than the $10 you paid initially. It should increase considerably, maybe to $15 or $20. You will be surprised to see your ETF's share price is trading way under $10 even when the underlying commodity of corn doubled and tripled in price. So what happened? See Figure 6.1 for the corn commodity and Figure 6.2 for the ETF corn fund.

Figure 6.1 Corn commodity 2013 - 2023

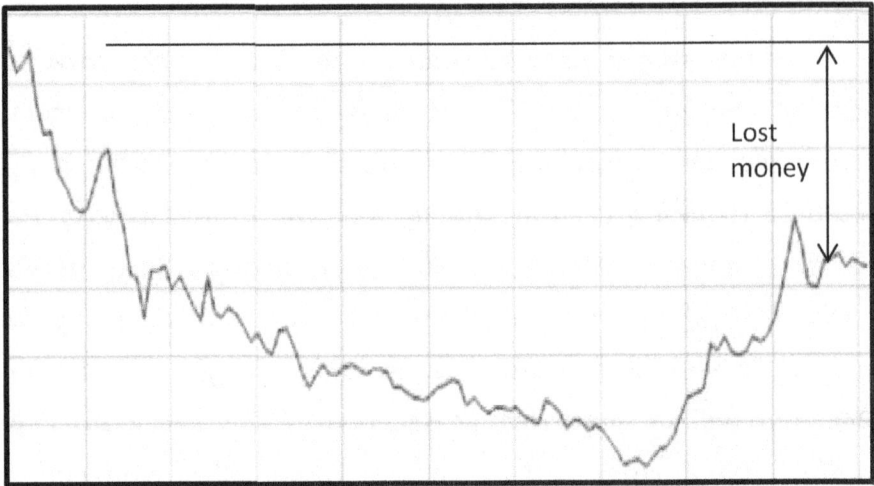

Figure 6.2 ETF corn fund 2013 - 2023

As time went by, your ETF was draining very slowly, day by day, your initial investment the way its share value was computed daily. Even when corn doubled and tripled from its bottom, your ETF's share price is still much lower. This is a terrible situation. If corn does not move up immediately, your investment will be drained. Suppose the ETF corn fund was trading at $20 at the peak of corn in 2013, that means when the corn commodity goes back to the same peak in 2023, the ETF corn fund should be trading very close to $20. However, as you can see from the chart of this fund in Figure 6.2, the share price was half what it was in 2013 even when the corn commodity is at its peak. This is a horrible situation. I hope you can see my point in this illustration and you spare yourself of being in such undesirable situation.

Some ETFs are designed with high leverage. For example, they trade an index or a commodity with a multiplier of 2 or 3. These ETFs are basically designed for gamblers and speculators. The ETF's share price is increased or decreased by a factor of 2 or 3 of the move of the underlying security. For example, if the underlying security moves down 4% on a particular day, the share price of the leveraged ETF by a factor of 3, would move down by (4% x 3 = 12%). If you are not right in a relatively short time on the direction of the security, your initial investment would be drained very fast. Yes, this is the disadvantage of some ETFs. I truly hope if you get nothing from this book, at least it would make you aware of this disadvantage and save you so much money and frustration in dealing with the market.

Remember! The objective of my system is to find an investment vehicle that will always come back. When we were analyzing an ideal and fair coin game, the problem was after betting seven times and doubling up our bets each time, the losses were so huge. We would also have been kicked out of the game. So to solve this problem, we need an investment vehicle that gives us the ability to stay in the game for as long as desired with the potential of this investment to always come back.

We also found out that an individual stock does not meet this requirement, and neither does an actively managed mutual fund. Options are shown to be just wasted assets when they are not used properly. So options, too, are not a suitable investment either. Commodities, while ideally, are great, practically are not suitable to be used in the system as well. One might wonder what else? Let us not get desperate. I had to go through all these types of investments to demonstrate the risk of using these financial instruments. Nevertheless, we still have an excellent alternative: How about the market itself?

Yes, the market itself! The market will not disappear for as long as our Western civilization exists. While all the investment types we discussed previously are not suitable applications for in the system, the market "collectively" exhibits the characteristics of a commodity. This is what I meant by the commodity concept. The market, as a whole, cannot go to zero. While some Individual stocks and companies come and go, new ones come and replace them. Society as a whole continues to evolve and creates "real" needs for different products, businesses, and technologies which always generate more supply and demand. Yes, the financial market "collectively" starts to behave like a commodity that will be always in demand and always supplied by the creativity and needs in society.

Hence, the market will always come back sooner or later. We can wait for it for as long as we like; hence, we will not be kicked out of the game. Unlike individual stocks, the market is already well diversified since it's a big basket of thousands of stocks. When I say the "market", I don't mean only the Dow precisely. I am talking in a general term. It can be a general index like, for example, the SP500. This index contains the largest and the best 500 companies in America. The "market" also implies the NASDAQ, which contains several thousand companies traded over the counter electronically. Another would be the NASDAQ100, which consists of the largest and the best companies in America, with many high-tech ones. Still, if you are more aggressive, but you don't want to gamble on individual stocks, you can use a sector index exclusively such high-tech index, biotech index, banking index, or energy index; a long list to choose from. You can trade these indices without the need to deal with the problems associated with the commodities themselves. Sector indices are definitely more volatile; this is a blessing to the system discussed in this book.

Now you might be wondering, how do I buy shares of the market or sectors in the market? There are several ways to do that. I am going to restrict my discussion only to what concerns the system in this book. There are many index funds out there, which track the underlying indices. These index funds exist in terms of mutual funds or ETFs. In other words, an index fund is not an actively managed fund with a fund manager betting on which stocks to buy and sell based on what that fund's manager thinks or chooses. A typical index fund runs on autopilot mode. Its objective is not to outperform the market. Its objective is simply to mimic the actual performance of the market or the sector with very minimum administrative cost relative to an actively managed fund. Ideally, an index fund will never outperform the underlying index taking into consideration the small fee associated with owning shares in it; it just mimics it.

Do you remember that I stated previously at the beginning of the book that about 75 to 85% of funds underperform the market? If you are outperforming 75 to 85% of the rest of the funds, year after year, that's a very good performance. Unlike an actively managed fund, there is no capital gain to be distributed by an index fund. Better than that, no whipsaws, and no missing big chunks of market moves while speculating on the direction of the market. These are the disadvantages of actively managed funds. None of that we should worry about in an index fund.

Since you will be always making a profit using the system on any sell order, you can always avoid paying taxes at the present by using a tax-deferred account such as an IRA or a 401K. Taxes, as you see, are not a problem anymore when you generate a profit. Of course, later on in life in your golden years, you will be paying some taxes in the wisest and most advantageous way at that time. What about commissions? Commissions should also be no problem at all. You can deal directly with the index fund company, you don't pay any commission for that. You really have no need to use a broker for that because you are not buying several actively managed funds and individual stocks.

Furthermore, you are already very diversified when you are buying the market itself. Nothing can be more diversified than the market. All you need is one or two index funds, that's it; you can buy them directly from the fund family, with no commission whatsoever. Well, what if you really like to trade these index funds during market hours like individual stocks? Sure, you can do that as well. Buy index ETF from a broker. Since you don't need any advice from a full-service broker, you can use very inexpensive brokerage firms that charge very few dollars per trade.

As you can see, you can save a lot of money in commissions, fees, and many other charges because you don't need any recommendations anymore. Many mutual funds come with a load; some also charge a percentage. You can avoid all that cost. Just be sure you use an index fund with a very tiny fee. Shop around!

Here we are, no taxes, for now, no commissions, no restrictions, and no need for other people's opinions. Does it seem like a perfect world? Now you might wonder, when are you supposed to buy and sell? Certainly, you don't want to speculate and guess like most market participants. Investing in an index fund already puts you automatically on top of almost 75 to 85% of the funds out there.

This seems to be a no-brainer; you really don't need me to invest in an index fund. This is where my system kicks in to turn the market into a business of buying and selling shares, not a casino anymore. The system is the brain that will generate all these buy and sell orders automatically without the need for guessing. You will learn about this system in the next chapter.

CHAPTER 7

DIGITAL MARKET MACHINE SYSTEM (DMMS)

Years ago, in an engineering graphic design course, we were supposed to learn how to draw manually a non-geometrical curve from another picture. The curve could be a face, a flower, or anything that does not have a geometrical form such as a square, a circle, etc. One might wonder why an engineering student should learn how to draw such a thing. Drawing a geometrical object with straight lines and angles should not be a hard task in engineering. But this task was to learn how to draw manually a non-geometrical object, such as a face or a flower. For an artist with great artistic skills and experience, that should be an easy task to do. However, most people don't necessarily have these artistic skills and such a task can be a challenge.

Nevertheless, the objective of that task was not to create artists from engineering students, but just to learn how to draw a random curve from another source scientifically instead of artistically. Surprisingly, the way to do that was much easier than I expected. All we had to do is to draw grids on the source picture and on the blank paper, then copy every grid individually by locating every element inside a grid to the corresponding grid on the paper. Careful measurements of the coordinates of every element relative to its grid produced a relatively accurate drawing of the object. Incidentally, even advanced artists use this technique when they are drawing on a very large surface, like a wall of several stories building. The grids help to keep the drawing in perspective and proportional since the human eyes fail to do that when looking at a large object from a very near distance.

How can a non-geometrical curve be relevant to investing in the market? If you look at any major market index chart, you would see that the chart somehow is a non-geometrical curve. You cannot locate a distant point by simply extending, expanding, or extrapolating any part of the chart, as is the case with a geometrical form. Hence, you cannot tell how the chart formation would be altered by the next move in the market. If you continue to follow the price change of the market day after day on the chart, you would be lost and confused more than ever. Drawing trend lines, and supports and resistances don't necessarily predict where the market would be going, and neither would eliminate whipsaws. Such technical tools just give a better picture of what already happened in the market.

If the market seems to be just a guessing game, you're certainly right. However, you need more than guessing, for sure, to tell where the market would move next. But since none of us has a crystal ball to predict the next move, the majority of people bet their hard-earned money solely on predictions and opinions. Unless you believe in true magic or have some supernatural power to foresee the future, all these predictions and opinions are not any better than your own opinions.

Fortunately, we don't need to predict or even know where the market is going in my system. Since we have no preference for a market direction, neither we have a preference for buying or selling, knowing where the market is going is basically irrelevant. Buying and selling, as I said previously, are equally important and needed. What matters more is to keep buying and selling. I am emphasizing "keep buying and selling" for a good reason. Sometimes the market becomes extended one way or another. That results in more buying or more selling when the market trends one way or another for an extended period of time. Nevertheless, the market always tends to react back and forth until it finds a more balanced level in the opposite direction to the extended trend.

Unlike all other systems out there, which assume a "know" position by trying to predict the market direction, the Digital Market Machine System (DMMS) assumes a "don't know" position and does not predict a market direction. This feature by itself takes all guessing out of the investing process and ends gambling. DMMS does not tell the market where to go, but simply it follows the market and produces automatically buy and sell orders accordingly. Since we love to buy as much as we love to sell, predictions and opinions are not needed. Whether the market goes up or down, it's irrelevant. There is a lot of wisdom when we drop our human arrogance and give back the market its deserved respect.

Recommendations are useless because we buy and sell "the market". Diversification is meaningless since we buy and sell the "whole market". What else could be more diversified than the whole market itself? Of course, one should not invest only in the financial market and ignores real estate, for example, and other tangible assets. However, this book focuses on the financial market part only. Although safety is relative in the investment world, there is nothing 100% guaranteed in the market. However, there is nothing also safer in the market than the market itself as a whole. DMMS, as shown, provides the most diversified and safest investment vehicle one can find out there.

Can DMMS become obsolete like all other systems? Absolutely not! As long as the market moves up and down, the system should continue to work as intended. In my humble opinion, as long as there are living human beings, supply and demand will always be generated and forming a "market" in one form or another. A typical system that assumes a direction in the market is bound to fail in the long run when a great majority of market participants becomes aware of it, anticipates it, and acts upon it. For example, let's consider the heating oil market. Seasons clearly play a major role and have great effects on how to trade this commodity.

For a novice trader, the most obvious thing to do is to buy heating oil during winter when demand increases during the cold season and sell heating oil in summer when demand decreases during the warm weather, right? However, through the years, traders became aware of this seasonal pattern. More traders started to use this seasonality as a "system" to trade this commodity. Hence, more and more people started to anticipate that and acted earlier and earlier until the "system" became obsolete. Simply, every year, traders try to buy heating oil earlier to catch the seasonal move before others. As a result of that, heating oil usually reaches its high often in summer instead of winter, Surprise? Similarly, the tax-selling season in the stock market often happens in late summer or fall, instead of December.

Why do all systems become obsolete? Well, as more traders become aware of a market action prior to a certain time or event, more traders try to apply it earlier and earlier to catch the move before others. These modified behaviors by market participants result in the loss of the effectiveness of a particular system. Any particular event or seasonality becomes well anticipated in the market; therefore, the market discounts it. The next time you hear someone telling you to buy heating oil in January, think about it twice. It's nothing more than a selling pitch to unaware and less experienced investors. Maybe it would be better to think about selling it short in winter.

Another popular example in technical analysis is the head and shoulders chart pattern. The expectation of many technicians and traders is to see the market breaking below the neck, at least a distance equal to the difference between the head and the neck. Since not everyone is a chart technician, the market sometimes moves as expected; other times, it does not. One may wonder what is the use of such a technical system when the odds are 50%. If you take a "true or false test", you will get about half of the questions answered correctly, even if you don't study at all. In fact, you would still get the same result even if you choose your answers randomly with your eyes closed and without reading the questions!

When a great majority of the market participants starts to expect the same move in the market, this move gets reflected and discounted by the market and the majority will be disappointed. Ironically, in a free market system, the majority is almost always wrong. Unfortunately for the masses and fortunately for the few, the market is not a democracy. The majority can always pay the minority, not the other way around. If the majority were correct, who's going to pay the majority? It would be impossible for the minority to pay the majority.

You may not see yet how drawing a random curve can be related to the market. Think about it, if you are not an experienced artist, you may find drawing accurately such a curve to be a difficult task. However, learning to draw accurately such a curve in a non-artistic way is very helpful, as I explained earlier. Similarly, if you find it quite difficult to predict where the market is heading next, DMMS provides a well-defined process with grids that produce these buy and sell orders automatically. This system will take out the guessing from investing as well as all the frustration that comes with it. In the long run, DMMS will beat the market and also the buy-and-hold investor.

How does DMMS do that? DMMS accomplishes that simply by "buying low and selling high" relatively. This is not a joke! I know that you heard that cliché so many times. The problem, as I described previously, is how low is low or too low and how high is high or too high? Low and high are relative quantities, but relative to what? If the market drops by 20% as it does from time to time then resumes its uptrend and reaches a new high, you may consider 20% a low and a lost buying opportunity if you do nothing.

However, what if you thought that 20% is low, but the market drops further to 50%? What if extreme global financial conditions and a depressed economy force the market to drop to 60% or 70% or more, as it happened in 1929 or the dot-com meltdown in the NASDAQ in 2001? I am not saying that the American market would drop that drastically very often, but the possibility is always there. Imagine how painful to be just a buy-and-hold investor in such a severe decline. But also Imagine how it feels to have a pile of cash to buy the market at such a huge discount!

Well, how does DMMS determine when to buy or when to sell without guessing? Buy and sell orders are triggered whenever a relatively low or a relatively high is reached, respectively. Notice I used the term "relatively" because no one knows how low is the actual bottom or how high is the actual top. In fact, as I already stated previously, the system assumes a "don't know" position. This is the unique feature of this system. With DMMS, you still can beat the market and make money even when you don't know whether the market is going up or down. The system also eliminates all emotional factors associated with market psychology such as fear and greed from interfering in the decision process.

Since DMMS uses the market as its investment vehicle, such a choice provides the best, the safest, the most diversified, and the highest possible odds of recovery and existence of any type of securities. In other words, if we continued to exist as a human species in a free market society, there is little doubt that the market would go to zero and would cease to exist. If we assume that our Western civilization would continue to exist for a long time to come, then it's somewhat safe to assume as well that the market would exist too. If we cannot make such an assumption, why should we worry in the first place about an investment when our human existence may cease to exist?

Hence, DMMS assumes that the market would always exist or at least would exist for a long, long time. Such an assumption puts the market always in the picture. We don't have to worry that the market would go to zero. The market in its entirety and collectively behaves like a commodity, which always reflects the natural supply and demand generated by society. So if our assumption is true, that implies the market would not go to zero; in this case, what else the market would be doing besides going up and down? Consequently, DMMS assumes that the market will always go up and down, but will never disappear. People will always buy and sell as long as fear and greed continue to be a part of their human nature. Therefore, the market will always fluctuate and will sometimes extend its moves in both directions, up and down.

Since we can assume safely that the market will always exist as long as humanity exists, then the market must always be somewhere in the picture. The question remains, as before, which way the market will move next? DMMS cares less whether the market moves up or down as long as it stays in the picture and keeps moving. I stated previously that buying and selling are equally important and needed. That implies the direction of the market is irrelevant. Therefore, we love the market, regardless if it's a bull or a bear market.

The question now becomes when do we buy or sell? Buying relatively low and selling relatively high is the answer. Well, how can we determine such "a relatively low or a relatively high?" If you have supernatural skills, and you can predict the future, you certainly don't need my system. Thus, until humans will be able to foresee the future, we still need a system or a mechanism for dealing with future events in the market. DMMS can provide this methodology to determine these relative lows and highs.

Like our example about drawing a random curve, if we don't have artistic skills, then we need "grids" to help us locate each point on the drawing. DMMS generates these grids mathematically, reflecting the highest odds of the best possible outcome. Consequently, DMMS would react in an exponential pattern as the market extends itself one way or another. For example, when the market moves significantly lower, DMMS starts buying. As the market moves aggressively lower and becomes extended to the downside, DMMS generates more buying orders and shares are accumulated at an exponential rate at relatively very low prices. Isn't it really a wonderful feeling to be scooping shares at the bottom?

Warren Buffett, the legendary American investor, once said: "be very fearful at the top and very greedy at the bottom". This is exactly what DMMS does. Most people act the opposite way by getting too greedy at the top and too fearful at the bottom. Of course, that's a disaster waiting to happen when people approach the market this way.

As a result of this exponential buying in a declining market, the average cost of the accumulated shares becomes significantly lower compared to what the buy-and-hold investor paid. If DMMS exhausts all its available cash on the downside, then a DMMS investor should feel very lucky, being able to accumulate many shares at very discounted prices. As the market starts bouncing back and moves higher, DMMS starts triggering sell orders, generating considerable profit on those accumulated shares all the way to the bottom.

The question that most likely comes to the reader's mind is what if the market continues to drop? DMMS addresses this situation by setting a safety factor at the start. This is a similar analogy to having an ahead start. I will explain in detail all the DMMS components in the next chapter, step by step. For now, let's consider the explanation in this chapter as an introduction or a general review of the system.

Investors often worry about a sudden and steep decline in the market. This would be a blessing to the DMMS investor. In this situation, the DMMS investor would buy as many shares as determined by the system and wait. Remember! The market will always come back sooner or later. This is why I introduced the commodity concept, it may take more or less time to recover, but the general market always recovers sooner or later. This is why DMMS does not invest in individual stocks or actively managed funds; these financial instruments might never recover. On the other hand, the general market behaves like a commodity. The natural supply and demand always bring the market back to its state of equilibrium.

Remember in physics, for every action, there is an equal and opposite reaction. Well, the reaction of the financial market might not always be equal, but a reaction would happen, and it can be more or less in the market terms. On the other hand, if you are simply a buy-and-hold investor who bought previously at a much higher price, you would be in pain for a long time to come. It may take years and sometimes decades, as I demonstrated previously at the beginning of the book. However, as a DMMS investor, even in such a market condition, the investor would be still buying and selling shares accumulated at the bottom of the market or during the fluctuations of the market generating a considerable profit even during a steep bear market!

Similarly, when the market moves higher, the DMMS investor starts selling some of these shares accumulated at lower prices. As the market moves higher and higher, the DMMS investor starts selling these shares more aggressively at higher and higher prices. The system generates these selling orders objectively, without the need for the investor to guess or to become emotional about that. When the DMMS exhausts all available shares as the market extends itself to the upside, a DMMS investor should feel lucky to have the opportunity to sell these shares at relatively very high prices.

Now, one might wonder what if the market keeps going higher. Again, this is why I don't invest in individual stocks or actively managed funds. No market will keep going higher in a straight line; sooner or later, supply and demand bring back the market to its equilibrium level. Fear and greed will always restore balance to the market as the overbought and oversold conditions are corrected. The DMMS investor would resume his buying activities again on retreating prices.

Well, what if the market moves sideways for a while? I am sure many readers have this question on their minds. Sideways don't mean the market would be frozen; the market would continue to fluctuate. The DMMS investor can still do some buying and selling on these fluctuations. Also, the cash portion of the capital to be invested would be earning some interest in a money market fund, unlike the buy-and-hold investor who would be making nothing meanwhile. In fact, the buy-and-hold investor would be hoping to break even at a higher price if his initial investment was made in a lump sum at a higher market price! Definitely, it is not a pleasant feeling for anyone to be stuck in a similar situation.

Basically, the DMMS investor keeps buying and selling depending on where the market goes with respect to the system gridlines. I will talk later about gridlines. For now, the DMMS investor does not need to worry about market direction, neither he needs to try to predict the next market move. Remember, I stated previously that, as a DMMS investor, I don't impose my opinion on the market and I don't need other people's opinions to speculate on the market direction. I simply let the market tell me where it's heading. I just follow the market. This is the beauty of this system. The DMMS generates the buying and selling orders without any guessing. After all, buying and selling are equally important and good, and that's what a business is about.

Since a DMMS investor would be always selling at profit, using the system in a tax-free or tax-deferred account would be a great idea to reduce or avoid taxes when possible while generating a capital gain. Most likely, the DMMS investor will rarely be 100% in or out of the market except in very extreme market conditions, the market will be always a business for such an investor. So the DMMS investor will always beat the market on the downside since the cash portion of his portfolio would be used to buy more shares at much cheaper prices as the market moves lower. This is the beauty of the system because it prevents certainly using all the cash from buying too early. Similarly, the DMMS will rarely sell all its shares too early as the market starts to move higher. Some of these shares are left to be sold at very expensive prices as the market keeps moving higher.

As time goes by, profit from buying and selling shares in addition to interest earned on the cash portion of the portfolio keeps compounding. As a result of that, the DMMS investor will always beat the market, and the buy-and-hold investor on the downside very easily. The DMMS investor also beats the market and the buy-and-hold investor on the upside, definitely in the intermediate and the long term.

As shown, whether the market goes up, down, or sideways, is irrelevant to this system. The DMMS investor is in the business of buying shares at wholesale prices and selling these shares at retail prices. Investing this way should always produce profit regardless of market direction since the market always fluctuates whether it's in an uptrend, downtrend, or sideways. Hence, while a volatile market is very painful for most investors, especially for the buy-and-hold investors, it would be a blessing for the DMMS investors.

Simply, the more volatile the market is and the wilder it swings, the faster the DMMS investor would be buying and selling shares and compounding more profit.

Ideally, if we can catch every move in the market and use 100% of our cash at the bottom of the move, then sell 100% at the top of the move, it would take a short time to become millionaires and billionaires. Realistically, however, that is impossible to do. Fortunately, it's partially possible with DMMS, and in the long run, will compound wonderfully on these market fluctuations. DMMS is that revolutionary approach to improving our investing methodology. DMMS is not an ideal or perfect solution, but it is a very realistic and practical solution designed to help us with our inability to foresee the future and deal with market uncertainties.

The system basically removes us from making investment decisions based on opinions, feelings, and speculation, trying to guess the next move in the market. The system takes into consideration a recent move in the market and analyzes it using various mathematical parameters to generate buy, sell, or just hold signals. In mild fluctuations, DMMS generates mild signals. However, when the market moves wildly, the system generates more aggressive signals taking advantage of such moves depending on the territories. The reason for these aggressive moves by the system is the fact that the market would not be able to sustain steep parabolic (almost vertical) moves, up or down, before returning to a level where it can find its equilibrium again. Hence, even when the market is going nowhere at the end except maintaining its level, these fluctuations become the source of generating profit all the time regardless of market conditions and direction. See Figure 7.1 DMMS buying and selling strategy.

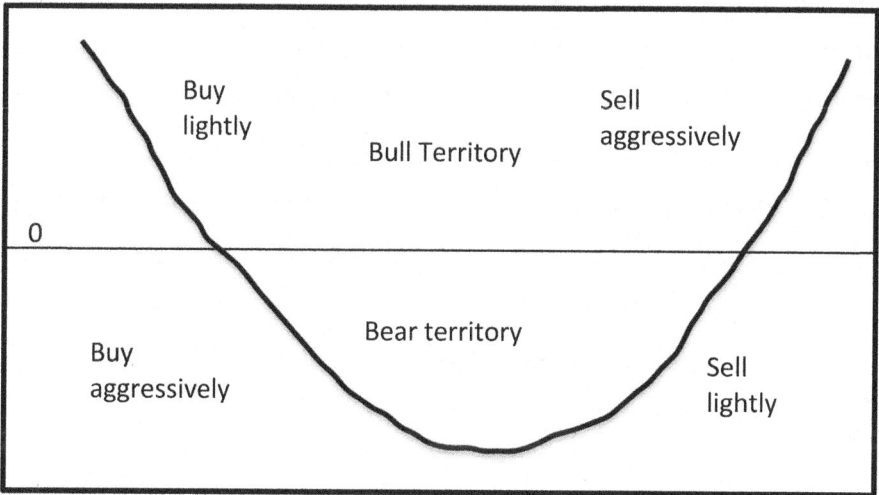

Figure 7.1 DMMS buying and selling strategy.

As shown above, DMMS takes advantage of all market conditions to produce a profit. When the market moves too far in bullish territories (+), the system will be selling aggressively its shares, as shown in Figure 7.1. When the market moves too far in bearish territories (–), the system would be buying its shares aggressively too, as shown in Figure 7.1. As I stated previously, DMMS buys its shares at relatively low prices and sells its shares at relatively high prices. During sideways and normal fluctuations, the system generates some mild buy and sell signals as well, producing some profit in addition to the earned interest on the cash portion of the portfolio while waiting for the market to make stronger moves in either direction.

When the market makes a wild move, up or down, DMMS triggers numerous market orders by buying and selling aggressively. Such wild moves are characterized by a strong possibility that the market would soon move in the opposite direction and return to a more balanced level. While many traders get whipsawed in such a volatile market and experience great losses, buy-and-hold investors worry about their holdings, DMMS investors would profit handsomely in such an environment and sleep well at night without the confusion and the worry that other traders and investors experience.

Buying during a down market and selling during an up market may not be the appropriate strategy for an individual stock or actively managed fund. Nevertheless, this strategy is justified when it's used for the market itself in combination with DMMS. As shown previously, that the general market behaves like a commodity and behaves according to the natural laws of supply and demand. So the market will always come back to regain its equilibrium as it digests other events and adjusts to new uncertainties.

I know many technicians and trend followers don't like to go against the trend. I agree with that partially. Unlike the buy-and-hold investor or a trader who tries to guess the entry point and invest his principal, DMMS starts to generate buying signal only after a sizable down move already takes place. Remember also that the system does not use all its cash at once when a buy signal is generated. If the market drops further, another buy signal would be generated. For those who are trying to catch the exact bottom, I wish them good luck! No one is going to ring the bell to tell you when the market reaches the bottom. Neither, the market is going to wait for you to jump on its wagon when it rebounds back immediately and unexpectedly. Even when one can catch the exact bottom, it's very easy to get whipsawed again if the market revisits its bottom and breaks through that level of support.

So long for trying to time the market! No one can, period. Timing the market is indirectly trying to predict a market direction. Predicting a market direction is another way of asking the market to move according to what we desire. Human arrogance and disrespect for the market can often lead to financial trouble in investing. That is certainly a very opinionated and biased view imposed on the market, which rarely produces any profitable results.

By using DMMS, we follow the market instead of trying to lead the market by imposing our views and opinions. There is wisdom and humility in this approach, as we recognize our human abilities. Those, who cannot swallow their pride, keep unsuccessfully trying to lead the market by imposing their opinions on the market. I don't believe anyone can be very successful in predicting what the market would do besides a few lucky times once in a while.

The purpose of this system is to assume a "don't know" position and never try to predict the market. Following such discipline would force the system user to buy basically when everyone is selling and to sell when everyone is buying. Isn't that the golden rule: buy when everyone is selling and sell when everyone is buying? This is what the system does. As DMMS investors, we would get greedy when people are fearful, and we would get fearful when people are greedy. Sure, sometimes it takes a lot of guts to practice this philosophy. It's not easy to do the opposite of what others are doing. DMMS would move its users from the crowd to the minority side. That is exactly what one should be doing, because the crowd is always on the wrong side in the long run. The majority pays the minority, not the other way around. Besides, the system does not jump in and out of the market, but moves in and out gradually in numerous steps. Therefore, the DMMS investor would never buy too late or sell too early.

I like to describe the market as a freeway where all investors are driving blindly, including us. In such conditions, since no one can see, the best way to change lanes is to start moving very gradually to the next lane instead of immediately. When two vehicles collide, they basically embrace each other from the side, avoiding a head-on collision that is more serious. Since the force components of the impact are mostly parallel to the vehicles, the effects of colliding would be less impactful. Of course, this is a very exaggerated analogy because all drivers cannot see, lanes are meaningless in this case.

DMMS immediately outperforms the market and the buy-and-hold investor on the downside all the time. The system undoubtedly outperforms the market in the intermediate and the long term. Unlike the buy-and-hold investor who would be painfully hoping to recover huge losses after the market drops aggressively, the DMMS investor would be buying shares very cheaply with peace of mind even when the market is in turmoil. Certainly, that is a big relief from the emotional stress associated with investing. Furthermore, the DMMS investor never worries whether to be in or out of the market, whether to buy or sell, or whether one is right or wrong on the market direction. All DMMS details will be shortly discussed in the following chapters.

"Buying low and selling high" is easier said than done, as I said previously. It's not easy to know how low is low or too low, or how high is high or too high. However, with DMMS aggressively buying on the downside at low prices and aggressively selling on the upside at high prices, one would be relatively buying low and selling high depending on the market moves and the territories. I stress "relatively" because the system would be catching most of the moves either way, without the need to time the market or inject opinions in the trading process, whether the investor is right or wrong on the market.

CHAPTER 8

STARTING DMMS

By now, we can understand and appreciate better the wisdom behind the built-in DMMS "don't know" assumption and the signals generated by its strategy in all market conditions. We now care less if the market is in a bull or a bear phase. If the market goes up, great! We make money by selling some shares. If the market goes down, great as well! It's an opportunity to buy shares at relatively cheap prices. We have no preference between these two outcomes since both of them are equally important and needed. If the market goes sideways, it's fine too. We still make some money from market fluctuations in addition to the earned interest from the cash portion of the portfolio. We don't need to guess, predict, or worry about the outcome. Dealing with the market becomes less emotional. Fear and greed have no effect on any buying and selling decisions. Such decisions are quantified and produced precisely and automatically by DMMS.

From the previous discussion, we know that if we can wait as long as it takes for the desired outcome to appear in a coin game at no additional cost, the game becomes very interesting and very profitable as well. We also know that gaining or losing sometimes comes in waves or cycles. Therefore, if we have the option to wait until our desired outcome appears, the dynamics of the game would change substantially in our favor. Although we cannot tell accurately how long the cycle will last and how great its amplitude will be, time becomes less relevant when we have the option to wait for our desired outcome. DMMS deals with the amplitude of the cycle, up or down. That may not sound realistic in a coin game; nevertheless, all these conditions already exist in a general market index as an investment vehicle.

Do we just buy and hold an index fund and forget about it? Of course not, though buying just an index fund put us ahead of almost 75 to 85% of fund managers out there immediately. But you're not reading this book just to learn about an index fund, of course. What would you do if the market declines steeply for a long period of time? That would be a very unpleasant outcome for the buy-and-hold investor. We would be sitting there maybe for years hoping that the market would recover. This is what the buy-and-hold investors usually do, they just hold. If for some reason, we bought the market at its top then a steep decline happens, we would be devastated financially and emotionally for a while, maybe for a long while.

We don't want to be just buy-and-hold investors for two simple reasons. First, it's very possible that the market moves against us at some time in the future and sits there for a long time to recover. Buy-and-hold is just another way of gambling, long-term gambling, making long-term bets. Second, we want to be active investors, and by that I mean, we should take advantage of the fluctuations of the market without the need to wait for the market recovery or play a guessing game.

Since a typical cycle has two major components, duration, and amplitude, once we can eliminate the effect of time, only the amplitude of these movements becomes our main concern. This concern is addressed by DMMS generating buy and sell signals to take advantage of these cycle movements. The objective of DMMS is to buy at a relatively low and to sell at a relatively high. This relativity is determined by the likelihood of certain moves in the market at various times. For example, if the general market moves up or down 30% in just one week, the likelihood of sustaining such a huge gain or loss would be very slim. All parabolic (almost vertical) moves correct themselves steeply sooner or later. So when such unusual movements occur, DMMS certainly would take advantage of them. For this reason, as the market becomes extended one way or another, DMMS becomes considerably more aggressive producing market orders in response to these unsustainable parabolic movements. Buying and selling this way comes as close as realistically possible to the true meaning of "buy low and sell high."

After understanding the general concept behind DMMS, it is time to get the nuts and bolts to assemble the details of this system. As I said previously, if you do not have the artistic skills to draw a random curve by hand, you may use grids to help you to do that. Similarly, if you don't have the ability to foresee the future and predict market movements (who does anyway?), you may use grids as well to locate these movements and respond accordingly. However, we are going to use different types of grids, so you should not worry about drawing anything.

Having laid down the many reasons why we should not be just buy-and-hold investors or speculate on the direction of the market, readers must be by now curious enough to learn the details of DMMS. I hope minor definitions and numerical figures would not discourage or bore you as a reader. After all, all market participants should have some appetite for numbers, since everything in the financial world is measured by numbers.

I will be defining and explaining every individual component of DMMS and its relationship to the system as a whole. Then, I will organize this information to be used practically in the real world. I will also demonstrate the system using an example with practical data to illustrate the use of DMMS. I would like to demonstrate the system using a very unpleasant and wild market, mostly in bear territory.

Applying DMMS to such an ugly market would certainly demonstrate the benefits of the system in difficult times, encountered in a very steep and painful bear market.

Demonstrating DMMS on a strong bull market would not serve much the interest of the readers. After all, who needs a system in a strong bull market when everyone is making money, right? Frankly, a buy-and-hold investor in a running bull market is not a bad strategy at all, assuming the bull would keep running forever. But we know, sooner or later, a bear will come out of its hiding and catches up with the bull. Blood will be running on Wall Street. During that time, the buy-and-hold investor would be in big trouble, while the DMMS investor would continue to profit.

DMMS is designed primarily for those tough times encountered in bear markets as well as bull markets. The system should always outperform the market and the buy-and-hold investor in bull or bear markets as time goes by. Having said that, I would like to caution the users of this system; there are no guarantees in the market. Past performance is not indicative of future results. There is always a possibility of losing money in investing. One should not invest before understanding the risk associated with any investment. Such a risk exists because no one can foresee the future or predict how other market participants would react to any particular event.

This is why the theme of this system is based on the "don't know what's next" assumption. The system should be only considered as an investing tool, keeping in mind that no tool is always the perfect and only tool. I have been using this system for many years, and I am very pleased with the results. That's why I decided to share that with other people as well.

Furthermore, the user of this system should remember that this system is designed to manage a portfolio, not a small individual trade. Everyone, once in a while, can be very lucky and double or triple a tiny amount of money spent on an option trade or a stock, but more than often, this small amount spent on the option can be lost and the performance of a stock can be disappointing. This is gambling, not investing. You can double your money in a casino as well if you make the correct bet, right?

What matters most in this discussion is the bottom line, the overall performance of your total portfolio relative to the market year after year. I doubt that many people can double or triple their entire portfolio year after year, as some people try to make you believe, when once in a while they double a tiny amount on an option trade. Genuine performance should be measured in terms of the total portfolio, not by, once in a while, a successful small individual trade. So if for example, you have $100,000 to invest, you would never buy one option or one stock with this amount, this is so reckless! You would buy a basket or several baskets of stocks. Your portfolio performance will be a fair comparison with the market performance. This is the purpose of DMMS to invest your total portfolio and to outperform the market year after year. The user of this system would especially appreciate this knowledge in a tough bear market.

We will move now to show how to apply DMMS in actual trading. First, as I said previously, this system is not designed for individual stocks, actively managed funds, or options. The first step in the system is to choose the financial instrument to which we can apply the system on it. The criteria for this choice must be that this investment vehicle would always come back as a function of natural supply and demand. An individual stock does not meet these criteria, since a stock may keep growing or declining for a long time and may even cease to exist altogether if the company's products become outdated or obsolete or face strong competition or any other reason.

Can we live without a particular stock? Of course, we can. Can we live without commodities from which our foods are produced? Definitely not. Similarly, an actively managed fund may not be suitable as well for our system for all the reasons I stated previously in this book. Unless you have a strong appetite for risk, even a narrow sector index might not be the best choice if you cannot tolerate much high risk.

While most people are impressed by the performance of the technology stocks in the market, using a very narrow technology sector, such as semiconductors, computers, software, internet, etc. A particular technology sector might not survive all the time. Technology changes often and can become obsolete fast. That is a risk that must be considered in choosing our investing instrument. While the individual sector is risky, the general market is much less risky in this regard.

For this reason, I personally prefer using a very general technology index, such NASDAQ or NASDAQ100. While companies can come and go and technologies can become obsolete, new companies also come into existence and new technologies are created. Modern society is always in need of new technological changes that meet the needs of the social changes. As a result of that, the general market will always be there to reflect these technological changes.

So what index should we use? I don't make any recommendations, but I can tell my readers what I personally like to use. Any investment vehicle should be used according to the investor's tolerance to the risk associated with the chosen investing instrument. Personally, I like to use NASDAQ or NASDAQ100 because they are very volatile, and I can tolerate the risk associated with this index. I also like the big moves, up or down, associated with this index.

I also like to use the SP500 or the SP100, which reflect the largest 500 and 100 American companies, respectively.

Therefore, I choose NASDAQ for one index fund and the SP for a 2nd index fund, which mimics these two indices as closely as possible with a minimum fee. This is my preferred choice for my personal use. This is where the ETF comes into the picture, so I can trade these ETFs representing NASDAQ and SP during market trading hours like any stocks.

Again, I cannot emphasize enough the importance of choosing the index fund ETF with the smallest fee. You certainly don't want the ETF's fees to drain your capital over the long term. Personally, NASDAQ and the SP are enough for me. Some people like to have more than two index funds. Some investors might think two funds only might seem a lack of diversification. Not true, remember I am buying the whole NASDAQ which contains thousands of companies, and the SP which contains hundreds of the biggest and the best American companies. So my portfolio is well diversified already. Other investors who can tolerate more risk can choose other index funds that reflect particular sectors in the market. It's really a personal choice and the ability of an investor to tolerate risk.

Rule #1,

Choose the market index you want to invest in, then choose the index fund that mimics your chosen index, depending on your personal tolerance to risk.

Once we decide on the market index we want to invest in, we will note the peak of that index. The peak might be an all-time high that was recorded years ago, or it can be a peak that has been reached very recently.

Rule #2

> Record the peak of your chosen market index; it's the all- time high value reached in the past or recently.

Having decided on the appropriate market index that accommodates our tolerance to risk and found an index fund that mimics our chosen market very tightly, we can move now to the next step in the system. The next step is to choose the appropriate value of the Safety Factor. Safety Factor also depends on our tolerance to risk. On a scale of 0 to 100%, zero being maximum risk and 100 being no risk, we choose the value that fits the investor's preference. Safety Factor is basically an ahead start. What do I mean by that? Well, I would wait for the market to drop a certain percentage before I initiate a DMMS position; so it's the initial drop that gives me an ahead start.

Having said that, it might not be still clear enough. A 0% drop means an investor can start immediately a DMMS position without any waiting period, which is, inherently, quite a bit of a risky start, especially if the market is at its peak. A 100% drop means an investor is willing to wait, ideally until the market is almost zero! (Of course, that's nonsense and not realistic at all because the market will not go to zero). I think you got the picture; it's basically somewhere between risk and no risk. So you decide how much risk you want to tolerate by deciding how much risk you want to start initially.

I personally like to have a drop between 25% and 35% or more if possible in the market before I start my DMMS position in the index I choose. A higher figure might take a very long time; I don't want to waste my time. So basically, I wait for a correction or a mild bear market before I jump. The DMMS investor does not need to trade frequently, only when there is a great opportunity. This is a great advantage to buy the index at a well-discounted price in addition to a well-diversified market. See Figure 8.1 illustrating an example of Safety Factor in the market.

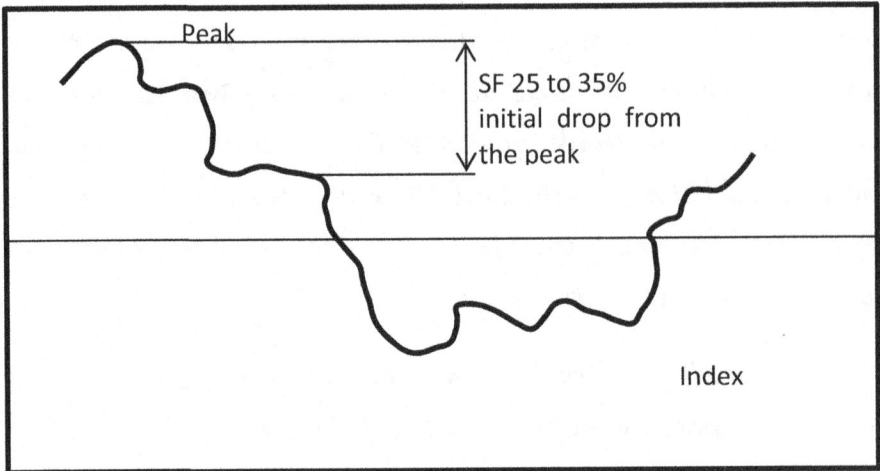

Figure 8.1 Example of an Index with SF%

Rule #3

Choose a value for Safety Factor (SF) with 0% (maximum risk) and 100% (no risk). Best when the initial drop is between 25% and 50% depending on your risk tolerance. The Starting Price would be at the grid line zero (the Neutral Line) or below.

Starting Price ≤ Peak - (SF% x Peak)

After we decide on the index we would like to use and find the corresponding index fund to which we can apply DMMS to it, we would decide on a value for the Safety Factor, the initial drop. Then, it's time to decide how much money we need to use for this DMMS position. This amount of money is referred to as the Starting Portfolio. This is the amount of money a DMMS investor would use to invest in cash and securities according to the DMMS rules. The amount will also be used as a reference when comparing the DMMS performance to that of the buy-and-hold portfolio's performance.

Note that the buy-and-hold invests this amount in a lump sum at the same time as the DMMS portfolio. Note also that the initial drop determined by the value of the SF% should be an immediate advantage for the DMMS portfolio only. But we are going to let the buy-and-hold portfolio use this advantage too. I would rather give an ahead start to the buy-and-hold investor by letting both portfolios start at the same time and with the same market value. Otherwise, the buy-and-hold would be already greatly underperforming the DMMS portfolio.

Rule #4

> Starting Portfolio is the total amount of money an investor would be using in a DMMS position, cash and securities.

Well, since the DMMS investor is not a buy-and-hold investor who invests his starting portfolio in a lump sum, the question that comes to mind, is how much the DMMS investor should start with? Since the DMMS assumes the "don't know" approach, that implies the DMMS investor must not start with 100% of the Starting Portfolio.

Otherwise, the DMMS investor would be acting exactly like the buy-and-hold investor, speculating on the market direction and imposing his views on the market. Therefore, the DMMS investor must start differently than the buy-and-hold investor. So how should the DMMS start? Another rule is needed to determine how much the DMMS investor should start with. This rule is the Risk Factor, which is a number between 0.25 and 0.50. For example, 0.35 represents 35% of the Starting Portfolio that remains in cash. 0.25 is for the most aggressive investor; 0.50 is for the most conservative investor. I personally like to use the number 0.35 which means I like to keep 35% of my Starting Portfolio in cash. Again, the DMMS investor should keep in mind how much risk is willing to tolerate.

Rule #5

Risk Factor (RF) is a number between 0.25 (aggressive) and 0.50 (conservative) of the Starting Portfolio that remains in cash for further use.

Formulas:

Cash = RF x Starting Portfolio

Securities = Starting Portfolio – Cash

Let's continue defining more components for the starting of a DMMS position. While that might seem to be too much work to make a trade, actually, this is not true at all. We are not making just one trade to buy one stock or one fund or one option for a few thousand dollars for a short period of time. It's only one position or at most two, for the entire amount of money designated for investment; that is, for the entire portfolio and for several years. So it's not too much work in terms of the entire portfolio.

One simple component is the Starting Date, as the name implies, it's the date when the DMMS initiates a new position and the buy-and-hold invests 100% in a lump sum at the same time for later comparison.

Rule #6

Record Starting Date for the DMMS position, which is also the starting date for the buy-and-hold position. This is the date when the market drops as determined by the Safety Factor

Obviously, we need Starting Price, which is the price of the share of the index fund that the DMMS and the buy-and-hold pay initially to start the investment after the initial drop determined by the Safety Factor. This is the price at which the buy-and-hold purchases in a lump sum the total shares of his portfolio.

Rule #7

Starting Price is the share price of our chosen index fund that the DMMS and the buy-and-hold portfolios pay initially to start the position. Note, the buy-and-hold uses 100% of its cash at this time to purchase its total shares in its portfolio. The DMMS' purchase is determined by the Risk Factor.

Now that we have the Starting Price, we can determine the total number of shares in the index fund when a DMMS position is initiated. Note, we use at this time the amount of money allocated for securities determined by the Risk Factor only in DMMS to buy the initial number of shares in the index fund for the DMMS portfolio.

Rule #8

DMMS Shares = (1 - RF) (Starting Portfolio) / Starting Price.
Where RF is the Risk Factor between 0.25 to 0.50

On the other hand, the buy-and-hold portfolio would use 100% of its cash at this time to buy the total number of shares of its portfolio. This amount is equal to the amount of the Starting Portfolio.

Rule #9

> **B&H Shares = Starting Portfolio / Starting Price**

Having introduced all the elements necessary in this chapter to start a DMMS position, I am going to summarize all this information in a table, so the investor can refer to it as the starting procedure for a DMMS position.

Table 8.1 Starting Table

STARTING INFORMATION FOR DMMS AND B&H INVESTORS			
Index	market	Starting Date	Date
Index Fund	Fund	Starting Price ≤ (1 – SF%)	
Starting Portfolio	Amount to be invested	Peak Where SF is between 0.25 and 0.50 (wait for a drop from 25 to 35% or more from peak to start)	

DMMS STARTING INFORMATION	
Peak	Peak of Market
Safety Factor	SF is between 0.25 to 0.50 Initial drop from market peak
Risk Factor	35% of starting portfolio remains in cash
Cash	To be invested in further market declines.
Shares	65% of Starting Portfolio / starting Price where 65% = 100% - 35%
Shares Value	Number of shares x Starting Price

B&H STARTING INFORMATION	
B&H Shares	100% of Starting Portfolio / Starting Price
Shares Value	Number of Shares x Starting Price

CHAPTER 9

THE DMMS NUTS AND BOLTS

Now what? We already learned how to start a DMMS position and see how it fares at the same time with an imaginary buy-and-hold portfolio in later on comparison in terms of performance. In this chapter, we need to dive into the details of DMMS, basically getting familiar with the nuts and bolts of this investing system. While the details of the system might seem overwhelming for the traditional investor or trader who is simply looking for a recommendation to buy a stock, a fund, or an option for a few thousand dollars, the DMMS investment approach is designed for a whole portfolio and for several years. Anyone can hit the jackpot once in a while by luck and make a good return on a small amount of money.

I am sure you heard a lot of these stories, especially in the options market, bragging about doubling and tripling a few hundred dollars on an option. Of course, you never hear about the many people whose options expired worthless. Nonetheless, in the end, what matters most is not a lucky small trade but the totality of the performance of the whole portfolio. Such a portfolio might consist of many small trades. You would see the combined performance of all these individual trades might not be as impressive in term of portfolio performance. After looking at the bottom line of the total portfolio, it might not be greater than a few percentage gain, if not underwater, not counting all the costs of trading in fees and commissions. Having a lucky small trade once in a while and having great results for the total portfolio are two entirely different animals. This explains why 75 to 85% of great money managers underperform the market every year.

The DMMS is a process that simulates a business of buying and selling shares in a particular market index for several years and using the entire portfolio in one or two positions in a couple of markets at most. So how do we proceed after choosing our market and buying a certain number of shares of an index fund at a serious discount according to our safety factor (the initial drop in the market)? Well, remember, according to our risk factor, we still have a portion of our portfolio in cash, right?

Does it really matter now if the market goes up or down? If the market goes up, we sell a portion of our previously owned shares bought at a much lower price. If the market declines, we use a portion of our portfolio's cash to buy more shares in our index fund at even much better prices. Voilà! Both outcomes are equally good, no worries and no sleepless nights. Now the question is, how do we decide when to buy, sell, or hold? Certainly, we don't want to guess, speculate, or inject our opinions into the market. That would be theoretically gambling and philosophically not giving the market its due respect by imposing our opinions on the market. Do you remember the discussion of the grids concept?

Yes, we go back to the grids concept. The market is moving continuously like everything else in nature during trading hours. So we need to set certain steps by digitizing the continuous motion. Do you remember our early discussion in the book about the continuous rotation of the earth and the growth of lawn? The continuous motion in the market is so confusing and compelling to many investors to speculate on the next move in the market. We will not do that. We will set our grids, the steps that make it clear to us to take an action, when to buy, sell, or hold without any speculation.

You can use the chart of your market index or the chart of your index fund to draw horizontal lines (gridlines) on it in a percentage term. The range of these percentages depends on really how actively and often you want to make a transaction. For example, you can assign a range such as 0%, 10%, 20%, 30%, etc. Zero is the Neutral line, 0%. So you assign these gridlines in a percentage term in both directions, to the upside and to the downside with gridline

0% being the neutral line, which is defined by Safety Factor. We refer to the upper side above the neutral line as the Bull Territory and the lower side below the neutral line as the Bear Territory. See Figure 9.1

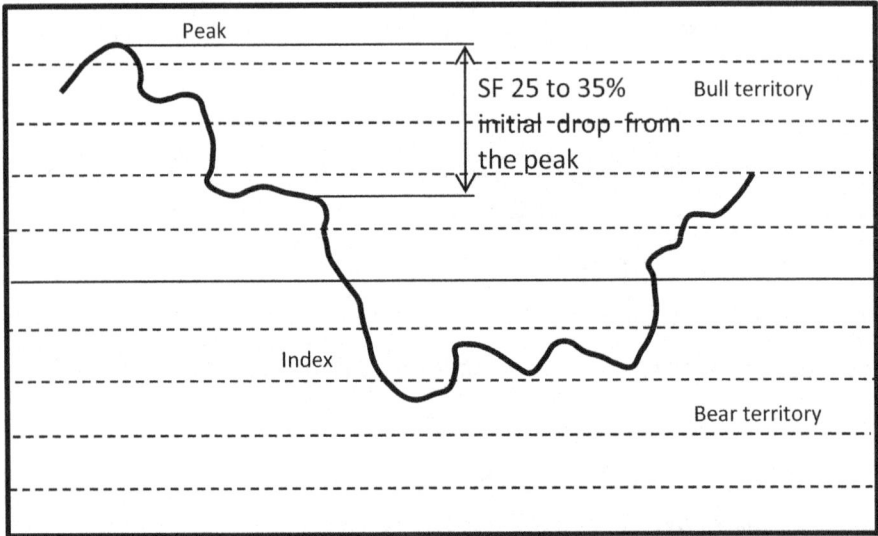

Figure 9.1 with Safety Factor and trendlines

Rule #10

Grids digitize the continuous motion of the market into well-defined horizontal lines. These gridlines are expressed in a range of percentages on the upside (Bull Territory) and the downside (Bear Territory) areas of the chart relative to the neutral line, 0%.

Bull Territory = above the Neutral Line 0%
    Gridlines: 0%, +10%, +20%, +30%, etc.

Bear Territory = bellow the Neutral Line 0%
    Gridlines: 0%, -10%, -20%, -30%, etc.

You really don't need to draw these lines if you don't want to. You can do that mentally by computing these range percentages on the chart of your index in the upside and downside areas. Furthermore, you simply compute the market values at +10%, +20%, +30%, etc. From the neutral line at zero on the upside. Then you do the same thing on the downside -10%, -20%, -30%, etc. from the neutral line at zero.

So now you have physically or mentally certain index values at which you can decide to buy or sell or just hold. When the market is fluctuating between two gridlines, for example between 10 and 20% but not crossing any gridlines, you do nothing. You just hold. You buy or sell only when the market crosses your gridlines. Simple, isn't it? That is crystal clear, no guessing or speculating, regardless of your feelings and opinion or anyone's opinion. When the price is between the gridlines, no action is needed, just wait until the price crosses your gridlines to act.

Do you see? You are not speculating anymore or imposing your opinion on the market. You give the market its respect by letting the market tell you what to do next. In other words, you are simply follwing the market instead of leading it. This is the beauty and the wisdom of the "don't know" approach. We don't use emotions and opinions; we don't make predictions and expect the market to comply with our desired outcome, not a realistic expectation. The market does what the market wants to do, irrelevant of what we wish or desire. We just follow the market; up or down is really irrelevant; both directions are needed and welcomed.

We know now when to act and when to wait. As long as the market is between the gridlines, we do nothing; we simply wait. The question that comes next to mind is, what should we do when the market crosses our gridlines? We know that when these lines are crossed, we should act; great, but how should we act? DMMS is designed to act lightly at small fluctuations, but acts aggressively when the market makes wild moves, up or down.

Remember our earlier discussion, we buy when everyone is selling; we sell when everyone is buying. That might contradict the trend-following approach, which is mostly a herd mentality approach, just following each other. In other words, we don't do what everyone else is doing. We don't want to join the crowd and be a part of this herd mentality. The crowd moves according to mass psychology. The market is not a democracy. The majority is almost always wrong; it must be this way. Because the majority pays the minority, not the other way around. So we're fearful when everyone is greedy; we're greedy when everyone is fearful.

Therefore, DMMS acts aggressively when the trend becomes extended up or down. We buy aggressively at the bottom of the market; we sell aggressively as the market starts peaking. Now, some readers wonder how can we know when the peak or the bottom is reached? The answer is we cannot. Imagine you are eating a fish; when you eat the whole body of the fish, does it really matter if you leave the head and the tail of the fish? Of course, the market is not a fish, but we should be grateful if we can buy aggressively close to the bottom and sell aggressively close to the peak even if we miss a tiny part of the peak and the bottom sometimes.

Some might wonder, but what if the market keeps going up or down? This is exactly why the DMMS never invests in an individual stock, actively managed fund, or options.

These financial instruments don't always come back. They might not follow the natural laws of supply and demand. We don't need a stock to live. That's why the DMMS uses only the market in its entirety. The financial market in its entirety starts to behave like a commodity. Commodities always follow the law of supply and demand; they never keep going in one direction. Humans need a market in their lives.

DMMS makes more money using fluctuations instead of trends. It's designed to buy at relatively lower prices and sells at relatively higher prices. Now that we understand well the concept of this system, how do we actually do that? Remember, our objective now is to buy or sell lightly at small fluctuations and to buy or sell aggressively as the market makes large moves in either direction. That's why we should always have some cash to buy at the bottom and some shares to sell at the top. Just like a business, you buy your merchandise at lower prices, and you sell them at higher prices. Both actions are welcomed and needed to conduct this business.

Furthermore, every time we decide to act whether to buy or to sell, we evaluate the DMMS Portfolio on that date and for that current price and compare its performance with that of the buy-and-hold portfolio.

Rule #11

> Record the date and the price when a market action is taken at which the DMMS and the buy-and-hold portfolios are evaluated.

Suppose we started a DMMS position in a particular market index at a discount price with a safety factor of 30%, the starting price would have been 30% or less at which we bought our shares. Remember also that we did not use all our portfolio's cash at that price. We used a risk factor of about 35%, for example. So we used 65% of our cash to buy those shares at the starting price. In this case, we still have 35% of the cash in our portfolio. We kept this cash because we don't know if the market would continue to decline after the 30% initial drop. So the Starting Price must be at or below our neutral line, the zero line. We compute and draw physically or mentally the gridlines on our chart.

Suppose now, for the sake of this example, the market continues to drop and it hits our -10% gridline. This would trigger a buy order. The question is how much we should buy? Since the market dropped initially 30%, then another drop of 10%, that's a total drop of 40% from the peak of the market. Realistically, the market might not drop more than 60% or 70% from the peak. Remember, we are dealing with the entire market, such as the Dow, the Nasdaq, the SP500, etc. So 3 or 4 gridlines in the Bear

Territory would be sufficient to draw. That would allow us to continue to buy shares down to about -70%. Similarly, we draw 3 or 4 gridlines in the Bull Territory. That would allow us to sell our accumulated shares all the way to about +70%.

The remaining cash in the portfolio would be determined by the Risk Factor, about 35%. Therefore, we still have that much cash after our initial buy at the starting price. This cash would be used to buy more shares if the market drops further. We can use, for example, 10% of our remaining cash once the -10% gridline is crossed by price. If the market drops further and hits our -20% gridline, we would be buying more shares with another 10% of the cash. If the price crosses two gridlines at once, we can use 20% of our remained cash.

If the market continues to drop, we continue to buy more and more at very low prices until we exhaust all our cash. For simplicity, you can use 10% of the cash for every time the market crosses down one gridline below the Neutral Line. These rules are not written in stone. You can be more aggressive at the bottom or at the peak, depending on your own tolerance to risk. Remember! The market will come back sooner or later as long as humans exist. Even if the market takes a long time to recover, you still can do some buying and selling on market fluctuations. So we should feel lucky if we can buy our shares at ridiculously low prices. This is the main reason why we invest only in the whole market. This cannot be true of an individual stock or actively managed fund.

Similarly, we do the same thing in the Bull Territory. Suppose, after the initial drop of 30% in the market, we use 65% of our cash to buy shares at a discount of 30% or more. If we are using a 35% risk factor, that means we still keep 35% of our portfolio in cash. We draw 3 or 4 gridlines in the bull territory, which will take us up to about 70%. if the market hits our +10% gridline, we sell 10% of the number of shares we purchased initially at the starting price. Suppose also the market keeps going higher and hits our +20% gridline. We sell another 10% of our remaining shares. If the price crosses two gridlines at once, we sell 20% of our shares, 10% for each gridline.

We continue to do the same thing until we exhaust all our shares. So for simplicity, we sell every time 10% of our shares for every gridline crossed by the advancing price above the Neutral Line. Isn't that wonderful to be selling shares at very high prices, when we bought them at very low prices?

This is what the DMMS is designed for. We are not doing what other people are doing. Notice, as the market goes down and people become fearful, we become more greedy and we buy aggressively. As the market keeps going higher and people become greedy, we become fearful and sell aggressively our shares at higher prices. We don't follow trends and we don't follow the crowd. This is mass psychology and herd mentality. We don't impose our opinions or other people's opinions on the market. We give the market its respect.

Likewise, we sleep well at night because we don't care which way the market makes its next move. We like to buy as much as we like to sell because we have no preference. We don't predict or speculate how the market will move next. Remember, our philosophy is "don't know". We are humble, and we just follow the market. Let the market do what the market wants to do, and let the market tell us what to do next.

To decide what market action we should take, we start always comparing the current price relative to the previous price. Depending on whether the current price went up or down enough to decide whether we should buy or sell and how much. If the price did not move much, no market action is needed.

Rule #12

> **Always compare current price to previous price to start to decide whether to buy or sell and how much.**

The question now is how high or how low should we wait before we decide to act without feeling that our decisions are too early or too late? The DMMS parameters are designed to sense and track market moves very closely and help us in the process of making such decisions. We use the gridlines as I explained earlier to decide the market action we should take. The current price might be less or greater than the previous price. I personally find gridlines on the chart to be very helpful in deciding the next market action.

Rule #13

Market Action Rules

<u>In bull territory,</u>

* Sell 10% of shares for every crossed gridlines by a higher price above the Neutral Line.

* Buy 5% of cash in shares for every crossed gridline by a declining price above the Neutral Line.

<u>In bear territory,</u>

* Buy 10% of cash in shares for every crossed gridline by a declining price bellow the Neutral Line.

* Sell 5% of shares for every crossed gridline by a higher price bellow the Neutral line.

It's really very helpful to see the big picture where we are during this process. Therefore we need to know here, for clarity, the all-time high of the market which would be the peak until it's exceeded by a higher price. In that case, the new higher price would become the new peak. For example, at the time of writing this book, the Dow was hovering around 32000, but the Dow reached previously an all-time high at around 36000. The current price, ideally, might be anywhere between zero and, 36000. Practically, however, it's almost impossible for a market to decline to zero unless our humanity and our civilization are coming to extinction for whatever reason. Otherwise, the market can drop drastically when it's over-extended or during economic and political instabilities. So a market decline of 70 or 80% is not something unheard of. The market can also reach a new all-time high as well, which would be considered the new peak for our system.

During the dot com era in the early 2000s, for example, the NASDAQ declined about 80%. During the financial meltdown in 2008s, the Dow declined 55%. Yes, these rare events are life opportunities and a savvy investor should be buying shares fearlessly. As we can see, the market cannot go to zero or below zero. Therefore, as we get so close to the bottom, the risk is greatly diminished. I would not say "risk-free" but it becomes so negligible in terms of the general market. Note that this is not the case for an individual stock or an actively managed fund or an option. These financial instruments can go to zero sometimes.

That's why DMMS does not invest in these financial securities.

By using a safety factor of 30% as an initial drop, for example, and keeping 35% of our cash, we have drastically reduced our risk on the downside. It's necessary to know where the current market value is located relative to its peak and zero. The reason we need to know where we are in this big picture is to be able to determine how lightly or aggressively our actions should be in dealing with the market. We already know that sooner or later according to history and to the natural law of supply and demand, the market is going to revert to find its equilibrium. Almost always, when the market becomes too extended one way or another, it would revert to its natural equilibrium.

Therefore, if we had the opportunity to buy some shares at -60% or -70%, and the market starts to revert, we should not be selling aggressively these shares once the market bounces back to just -50%. At such a small bounce, we should be selling very lightly at this time, or not at all. We know the market has the potential to bounce back much higher toward the neutral line, the zero line. Then, we gradually become more aggressive in selling the shares that we accumulated at the bottom of the market near the lowest negative gridline. Certainly, we should be selling aggressively as the market keeps moving higher in the bull territory toward the established peak. We continue to sell aggressively at this level while the market keeps going higher until we exhaust all our shares.

If the market moves beyond the previously established peak, then we readjust the neutral line, the Gridline zero. Remember, we created this line using the Safety Factor (25% to 50%) initial drop from the peak to start our DMMS position. When the market reaches a new peak, this neutral line (zero line) must be readjusted. We use the same Safety Factor, for example, 35% from the new peak to obtain our new neutral line.

This is the beauty of the DMMS because it adjusts itself as the market moves higher and goes beyond the previously established peak. This way, we don't get kicked out of the game; we just readjust and continue the business of buying and selling shares. So we define the gridline of our Neutral Line, zero, as:

Rule #14

> Gridline 0% = New Peak - (%SF x New Peak)
> where Gridline 0% is the new Neutral Line.

I should mention that the neutral line or the Gridline zero is adjusted only when the market reaches a new peak. No need to adjust the Neutral Line on the downside because the market is limited by its bottom at zero. The market can never go bellow zero and most likely never zero. So now we know how to adjust our Gridline 0% as the market exceeds its previous peak. Obviously we should be selling aggressively at these higher prices.

But how should we be selling once the market reaches its low and starts to bounce back? While the market is still in the bear territory, meaning bellow the Neutral Line, selling must be very light. I personally sell no more than 5% of the accumulated shares as the market crosses a higher gridline bellow the Neutral Line, for example from -50% to -40%. I would not be selling aggressively bellow the Neutral Line knowing that the market has the potential to go much higher later on.

Of course the market will never go straight up; it might fluctuate for a while or even revisits its established previous low. That's why we try to do some light selling even in the bear territory to make some money from these fluctuations during bearish periods. These selling transactions take place as the market moves between the negative grid lines. Note during this time, the buy-and-hold investor would be miserably waiting for the market to recover or just break even at the starting price, while the DMMS investor would be making money even in bear territory and accumulating more shares and some accrued interest on the cash portion remaining in the DMMS portfolio.

The gridlines are very useful way in the system that shows us where the current price is in the big picture between the peak and the bottom. These gridlines give us a clear view and the likelihood of any probable further move by the market in either direction. Remember the ball analogy? After an extended move upward, the ball would start to slow down ascending until it comes to a complete stop and reverses immediately its direction, then it starts falling down fast. The market, sooner or later, tends to go toward its equilibrium state especially after wild moves, up or down.

These gridlines would be used as our guidance in our market actions depending where the current price is. In the bear territory (bellow the Neutral Line) we should be buying shares aggressively and sell lightly some shares while the market fluctuates. We would do the opposite in the bull territory (above the Neutral Line), we sell aggressively these accumulated shares and buy lightly when the market fluctuates.

Now some might wonder how aggressively or lightly we should be acting. I thought about quantifying these market actions, but I do realize it's an individual choice depending on our personal tolerance to risk. Personally, I make it quite simple, I quantify aggressiveness by 10% and lightness by 5% of my market actions as shown in market orders depending whether the price is in bull or bear territory. This way I would be able to spread my cash and my shares over a relatively wide range. But again, this is not something to be considered written in stone. My book is about sharing my concept of investing, not about imposing rigid rules on others.

There are times when DMMS does not generate any buy or sell orders; instead, the system chooses to do nothing. The reason for that is we do not want to buy too soon before a considerable decline, nor do we want to sell shares too soon as well before a major advance. While a "do nothing" alternative takes place, we simply wait until the market makes up its mind one way or another. Remember, do nothing is not a bad thing when using DMMS as a way of investing. The cash portion of our portfolio would be still earning some interest while the market is going nowhere. On the contrary, the buy-and-hold portfolio would be earning nothing regardless of the length of time since all its allocated cash was used at the start in securities.

We move now to the most interesting part of the DMMS, the bottom line. A system is useless if it does not yield some advantages over its competition. Therefore, we need to evaluate the performance of our DMMS portfolio relative to the buy-and-hold portfolio. The buy-and-hold usually reflects the market; but in this case, we are giving the buy-and-hold in our analysis an ahead-start when we let the buy-and-hold purchase its shares at a discounted price at the Starting Price, during the initial drop of 25% to 35% recommended by DMMS rules. Remember, the Safety Factor is a very essential part of the DMMS.

So we start by computing the value of the DMMS portfolio by adding the shares value plus any cash and any accrued interest on the cash. Note that Shares Value can be obtained by multiplying the number of shares by the current share price for that period. After computing the value of the DMMS portfolio, we figure out the DMMS Return by computing the current value of the DMMS portfolio relative to the DMMS starting portfolio in percentage terms. Don't worry for now about all these calculations. Next chapter, I will be going through every detail and show all computations to make sure everything is very clear and easy to do.

Similarly, we compute the value of the buy-and-hold portfolio by multiplying its number of shares by the current share price for that period. In this case, the buy-and-hold portfolio contains only securities with no cash or earned interest. Remember, the buy-and-hold used all its cash initially to buy its shares. To compute the return of the buy-and-hold, we compare the current value of its shares relative to the starting value of those shares purchased initially at the starting price in percentage terms.

Finally, we come to the critical moment, which is comparing the two portfolios, the DMMS portfolio, and the buy-and-hold portfolio. The performance is shown in the difference between the returns of these two portfolios. If the value of the DMMS portfolio is greater than the value of the buy-and-hold portfolio, then the DMMS portfolio would be outperforming, and its performance would be expressed in a positive percentage term. On the other hand, if the DMMS portfolio return is less than the return of the buy-and-hold portfolio, then the DMMS portfolio would be underperforming and performance would be expressed in a negative percentage term. Note that either or both portfolios' returns can be negative at a particular time. The less negative return would be the outperforming portfolio, since subtracting a negative number would be actually adding that number.

Rule #15

DMMS Portfolio = shares value + Cash + earned interest.
Where shares value = shares x share price.

DMMS Return = ((DMMS portfolio - DMMS starting Portfolio) / DMMS starting portfolio) 100%

B&H Portfolio = B&H shares x share price.

B&H Return = ((B&H Portfolio - starting B&H Portfolio) / starting B&H Portfolio) 100%

Performance = DMMS Return% - B&H Return%

Having gone through all such details in defining the DMMS components, that might seem a little confusing or too involving. In reality, we don't have to do that much, only once a while, maybe once a month. We take a look at the market from time to time to see what the market has been doing, then decide what action we should take, if any. This portfolio review can keep us well-informed and involved in the market without trying to speculate on the market direction or letting emotions and opinions run high. We let the market tell us what to do next. We never impose our views on the market. This is the beauty and the wisdom in this system. I end this chapter by providing a table summarizing all the needed information to periodically evaluate the DMMS portfolio and compare it with that of the buy-and-hold portfolio.

Table 9.1. A Periodic Evaluation Table

DMMS PARAMETERS

Date		Peak	
Price		Crossed	
Previous Price		Gridlines	

Table 9.2 Market Orders

Bull Territory (Above Neutral Line)		Bear Territory (Bellow Neutral Line)	
Price > Previous Price	Sell 10% of shares for every crossed gridline.	Price > Previous Price	Sell 5% of shares for every crossed gridline
Price > Previous Price	No Action if no crossed gridlines	Price > Previous Price	No Action if no crossed gridlines
Price < Previous Price	Buy 5% of cash in shares for every crossed gridline	Price < Previous Price	Buy 10% of cash in shares for every crossed gridline
Price < Previous Price	No Action if no crossed gridlines	Price < Previous Price	No Action if no crossed gridlines

Table 9.3 Transaction Table

Info Before Transaction		Info After Transaction	
Date		Buy Order	
Price		Sell Order	
Market Action		Shares After	
Cash Before		Interest Earned	
Shares Before		Cash After	
Transaction		Shares Value	

Performance			
DMMS Portfolio Value		B&H Portfolio Value	
DMMS Return %		B&H Return %	
Performance	DMMS Return % – B&H Return %		

CHAPTER 10

PUTTING DMMS TO THE TEST

How does DMMS fare if we put it to the test? This is what this chapter is about. After all, what good a system is if we cannot make money with it and does not provide some protection in difficult market conditions? It's like having a computer with no monitor and no keyboard. Regardless of how fascinating a computer is, it's worthless if we cannot have a way to input data and have no access to the output which facilitates our data processing task. So let's put DMMS to the test and see how good really it is.

How do we test such a system, or as a matter of fact, any system in general? Ideally, the best test for anything, in my opinion as an engineer, is to apply the worst case and then see how the tested object would perform under the worst conditions. Realistically, however, that is not very practical or useful in real life. Imagine, for example, car companies doing a collision test using the worst case, say, 150 mph speed in bad weather conditions. What would that test tell us? Nothing! Certainly, every car out there would end up with disastrous results, regardless of how good that car is. For this reason, car companies do their collision test on their cars using low speeds, about 30 mph, and in good weather conditions, then we can compare different cars using the same test. That would be a more useful collision test practically, but definitely not the worst case . Similarly, we don't expect the construction industry to test their buildings using a simulated earthquake of 10 on the Richter Scale. Everything that is standing out there would collapse in such a powerful earthquake. However, construction companies expect their buildings to survive milder quakes, somewhere between 6 and 7 on the Richter Scale.

So what is the worst case that we can apply in testing DMMS? Since we are buying a market index and not selling short that index, the only way to make money, in this case, is for the market to go up. Ideally, the worst case would be then a market index that keeps going down forever. But we know that markets cannot go below zero, and not even to zero. Frankly, I would not like to choose a milder test on DMMS because I hate gambling and losing money. So I am going to apply the worst case: a bear market forever!

A bear market forever? Yes, and this is not a joke. Let us try that on DMMS to find out how it would handle such a remote possibility. First, is it possible to have a bear market forever? Of course, if you own an individual stock or a bunch of them, they may keep declining until they go finally to zero and stop trading. That money would be lost forever in such stocks. But what if you own a fund? The odds improve in this case since a fund consists of many wisely selected stocks, sometimes more than 100 of them.

Nevertheless, when a fund is an actively managed fund, the fund manager most likely is guessing and betting on a particular direction for every stock in the fund portfolio. Like most market participants, such a fund manager is getting whipsawed as well and the fund value would be eroding gradually and underperforming the market index, as it's the case with 75% to 85% of mutual funds underperforming the market every year.

Now, you maybe are wondering if it's possible for a fund to go to zero. It's extremely unlikely for a fund to go to zero, not only because it's a basket of many stocks, but because it's possible for the fund to avoid that outcome or even the appearance of it. Simply, when the net asset value of a fund goes drastically low, the fund would do a reverse split to bring back the share price to a normal level and attracts fresh money through advertisement. If, for example, the fund raises its share price by a factor of two, the number of shares is reduced by a factor of two. For example, if you own 200 shares of a fund at $5/share, you would have 100 shares at $10/share. That's how the appearance of normalcy is maintained. The unsuspecting new investors might not be savvy enough or aware of this trick, thinking all is just fine.

So the fund continues to operate normally without the appearance of its poor performance. Of course, a savvy investor can do further research and find out the true performance of the fund.

How does DMMS fare if we apply the worst case? Can it go to zero? There is no doubt that DMMS would immediately outperform the buy-and-hold investor if the market declines. This is a built-in feature in the DMMS. Ideally, a buy & hold investor uses 100% of his allocated money to buy shares in a particular security in a lump sum and hold that position for an indefinite time, or at least for a long time. Otherwise, if this investor tries to time the market and buys at different times, then he's no longer a buy-and-hold investor; he would be more of a market timer or a trader.

On the other hand, a DMMS investor uses only a portion of his portfolio's cash to buy securities determined by the Risk Factor, as shown previously. This Risk Factor is a number between 0.25 and 0.35 depending on the investor's tolerance to risk, meaning that the DMMS investor is still holding 25% to 35% in cash. When the market declines, if we're using 35% in cash, the DMMS would be buying more shares at lower prices while losing only on the 65% invested initially in securities and earning some accrued interest on the cash portion. On the contrary, the buy-and-hold investor would be losing 100% of his portfolio hoping and waiting that the market would come back while not being able to collect any interest since his cash portion is zero. As you can see, a DMMS investor would always outperform the buy-and-hold investor in a declining market without any doubt.

Beating and outperforming the buy-and-hold investor is a nice feeling, but certainly, we don't invest and risk our money just to beat someone else's performance and prove a point. We invest simply to make money. So does DMMS go to zero? The answer is NO, unless you believe the market itself can go to zero.

Does the market go to zero? I let you have the final answer to this question while I express my reasoning and opinion regarding this matter. Individual companies come and go depending on how much their products and services are needed and whether they can survive the competition. Their corresponding stocks also come and go out of the market. However, the market always exists regardless of what stocks go in or out of it. In my opinion, the market will always exist as long as we have a free market system; as long as our western civilization exists; and as long as life and humanity exist.

No one thinks that corn, wheat, or gold would ever go to zero since the need for these commodities will never stop. Similarly, the stock market represents the value of physical and intellectual assets to sustain our livelihood and growth as a society and human beings. Technology keeps changing quickly, but we will always need technology in one way or another in tackling problems and ways of life. Medical services and drugs continue to change, but healthcare will always exist as long as life itself exists on this planet and people get sick and age. The market will continue to exist because life and its physical needs bring the concept of supply and demand. The market is the most efficient way to express supply and demand in a world managed by humans.

Thus, the answer to whether DMMS can go to zero is intimately related to the survival of the market itself. Hence, a DMMS portfolio can survive the ideal worst case of a bear market forever, since no bear market can take place forever in the general market. Remember, that is not a true statement when an individual stock or an actively managed fund is used for the reasons I discussed previously in this book.

If a forever bear market cannot likely take place in the market, then what would be the next worst case to test for? Would a very steep, volatile, and lengthy bear market be the next worst case? What market can we use as a real-life test for our system? Definitely, no one would care to use a system unless an investor is not sure what to expect from the market and needs some protection along the way dealing with the market. Therefore, no need to test DMMS in a pleasant bull market. We are left with one choice: a volatile and steep bear market, which is scary and unpleasant to any investor.

It was Year 2000, yes over a couple of decades ago, the dot com era. Internet stocks were flying high, and the world was experiencing a new era in connectivity and social media. It was during that time I started working on the DMMS. The financial market was going crazy, and the internet stocks were defying "gravity" and all logic. They were flying high for a reason or often no reason, then they came down as fast, crashing down to nothing except very few companies. A year later, the Nasdaq came down drastically, about 80%.

People did not care how high the market was; they just wanted to jump on the wagon, thinking the market would continue to go higher. Isn't it always the case in a bull market? In fact, any market, including a bull market in real estate. Nonetheless, the financial market of Year 2000 came down crashing. The Nasdaq lost 80% during that time. It took the Nasdaq 15 years to break even and reach its previous high of the Year 2000, around 5100. Imagine being a buy-and-hold investor stuck in such a bad investment for 15 years just to break even.

It was during that time, I realized that many people were treating the financial market as a casino. It was not a place to make bets for entertainment, but a place to gamble with their hard-earned money, letting their emotions and opinions swing between their fear and greed. I realized there must be a better way to approach the market. During that era, my DMMS was born. So I was looking for the worst market to test my system.

The best "worst" market was the gold stock index at that time. While the internet stocks were flying high, the gold stocks were performing horribly. So during that time, I started testing the DMMS using the gold stock index. For those who swore by gold, they were more than disappointed during that crazy time of the dot com era. They thought gold had a better value than those internet stocks full of just "hot air". Logically, they had a good point. Nonetheless, market participants often act on expectations. The gold never made any move during that time. A buy-and-hold gold investor was suffering disastrous results during those years.

As I said previously, I needed to test my DMMS on a very bad market. So I found the gold index to be the market for my test at that time. By the way, the symbol of this gold index is XAU, which represents the blue chip gold stocks for North American major gold companies. I used one decade of data on this market as a real-life test. The results were more than amazing, and I adopted this way of investing for the next 20 years. I was very pleased with the results. So I decided to share my system with the world before my time on this earth expires. Since there is no "forever" bear market, I decided to create the next worst case for this test, a very unpleasant and wild market, to illustrate more effectively this system to my readers at the time of writing this book.

Since I don't make recommendations in my book, I decided not to use any securities names for my illustration. After all, the purpose of this book is to explain the concept of this system and share my thoughts and experiences with others. As you can see in Figure 10.1, the chart shows a very unpleasant bear market fluctuating up and down wildly mostly in bear territories crossing a few times to the bull territories and then declining again. My objective was to simulate these undesired market conditions to be able to effectively illustrate the concept of this system as clearly as possible. Therefore, I am going to show step by step how to apply this index fund in testing DMMS and compare its performance with the market's performance represented here by an imaginary buy-and-hold portfolio.

Having found an appropriate test to examine our system, let us start this process, illustrating all the necessary steps using the chart shown in Figure 10.1. While this chart does not represent an actual fund, it really makes no difference, since all markets fluctuate anyway. I also wanted to include the bearish, the sideways, and the bullish periods to see how the system will perform in all market environments. The wild fluctuations will be applied to both portfolios, the

DMMS Portfolio and the Buy-and-Hold portfolio, then we'll compare their performances side by side.

So we will see how DMMS would fare using such a "lousy" market. While we can see already the previous, current, and future prices on the chart, remember, in real-time we cannot see the future prices. We trade from the right side of the chart, which means, we can never see what will come next on the chart on the right side until that move becomes the present and the past.

To make it more practical, let us assume that we have $100,000 to invest in each of these two portfolios. The same amount would be used in the DMMS portfolio and the imaginary buy-and-hold portfolio. Then we'll compare the performance of these two portfolios as time goes by. At the time of writing this book in 2022, I have been using DMMS for almost 22 years as my investment style, and I am more than satisfied with the results. So this is beyond theoretical assumptions; this is a real-life experience. This is why I decided to write this book after more than a couple of decades. Therefore, I am going to proceed step by step in illustrating this concept of investing using the data shown on the chart for this test.

Figure 10.1 Testing Chart

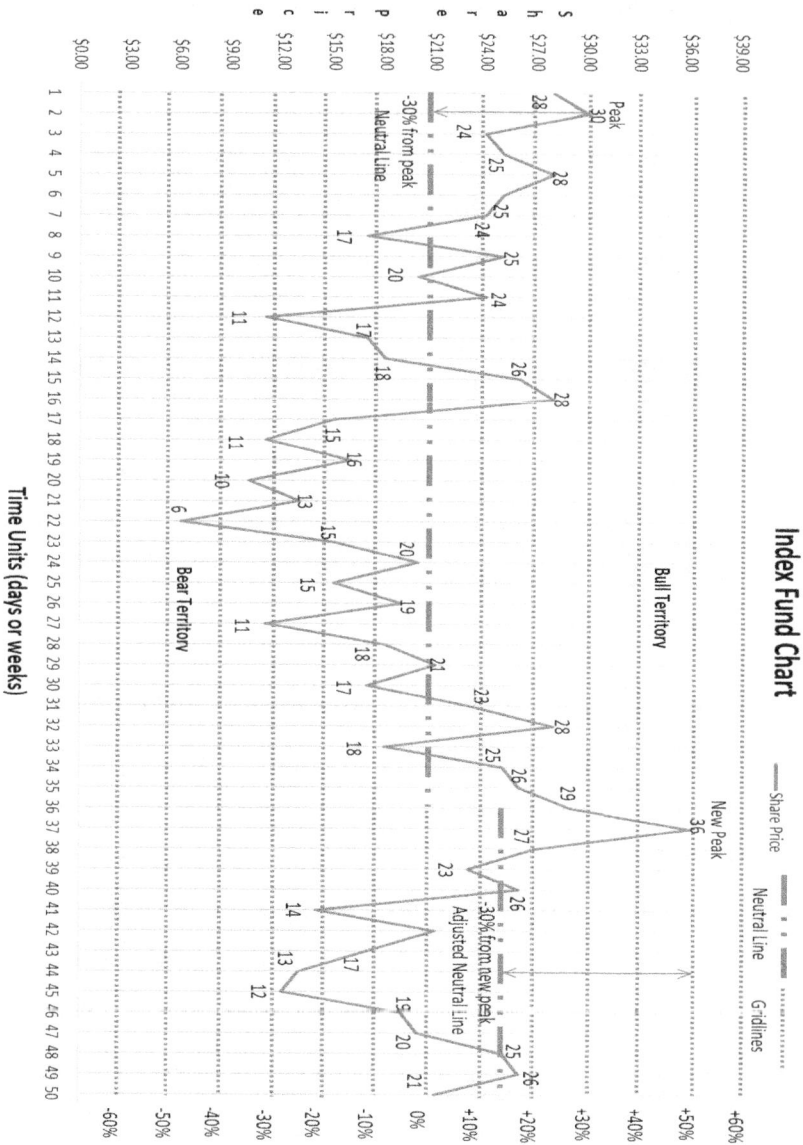

Index Fund Chart

Share Price — Neutral Line — Gridlines

Share Price ($): $0.00, $3.00, $6.00, $9.00, $12.00, $15.00, $18.00, $21.00, $24.00, $27.00, $30.00, $33.00, $36.00, $39.00

Percentages: -60%, -50%, -40%, -30%, -20%, -10%, 0%, +10%, +20%, +30%, +40%, +50%, +60%

Bull Territory

Bear Territory

Peak

New Peak

Neutral Line

-30% from peak

-30% from new peak

Adjusted Neutral Line

Data points: 30, 28, 28, 24, 25, 25, 24, 24, 20, 17, 18, 17, 11, 11, 10, 6, 13, 15, 15, 16, 20, 19, 18, 17, 21, 26, 28, 28, 29, 25, 26, 27, 36, 23, 26, 25, 26, 14, 13, 12, 17, 19, 20, 21

Time Units (days or weeks): 1 2 3 4 5 6 7 8 9 10 11 12 13 14 15 16 17 18 19 20 21 22 23 24 25 26 27 28 29 30 31 32 33 34 35 36 37 38 39 40 41 42 43 44 45 46 47 48 49 50

Since we are using $100,000 as a virtual portfolio, and since some of the DMMS portfolio remains in cash, it's important not to forget that this cash would be sitting somewhere earning some interest while waiting to be invested. But for the sake of simplification, interest accrued will not be added to the process for now. In the real world, that part of cash would be earning some money, which would be shown in the investor's account. This is another advantage of the DMMS compared to the buy-and-hold investor who would not be earning any interest since this portfolio would be 100% invested in securities. An interest of 3 to 5% is not a bad thing while waiting for the market to recover from a bear market. Practically, we don't need to compute that because the financial institution provides that periodically.

Next, we start filling in the starting information of both portfolios. We already have the test chart of an index fund, which mimics very closely an imaginary market index. From the index fund chart shown previously in Figure 10.1, we can see that we have 50 time periods with their respective prices in our data. These time units can be considered days, weeks, or even months if you like. It would make no difference for the purpose of this illustration, since we are not computing the accrued interest in this test. We already decided to ignore that interest to keep things more simple. So think of the time unit whatever you prefer. Realistically, the market rarely makes such wild moves in a very short time or in equal time units. But we are using this chart simply for illustration.

For the next step, we should have a starting date and a starting price. In order to have that, we must apply the Safety Factor Rule, an initial drop from the peak of at least between 25 to 35%. If we get a lower drop than that, it would be even better. I usually use 30% for the Safety Factor where I draw my Gridline 0%, the Neutral Line. So we have to note the peak while waiting for the initial drop.

We can see from our chart that the shave value went from $28, then to $30, then it started to decline further. So we record in our table $30 as the peak and wait for a minimum initial drop of 30% or better. If the market goes to a higher new peak, then the new peak would be used for the calculation. In this case, the market dropped below 30% during time unit 8 to $17. We have now our Starting Date and Starting Price and our Neutral Line (Gridline 0%) at - 30% from the peak price of $30 which would be $21. We enter all that information in our table.

Now, the next step is to start our DMMS position. Remember another very important rule, the Risk Factor, which is the amount of cash that remains in the DMMS portfolio. The Risk Factor should be between 25 and 35% as well. Since I am a conservative investor, I chose to keep 35% of the portfolio in cash. Thus, 100% - 35% = 65% allocated for buying shares in the index fund at $17. The number of shares for the DMMS portfolio is computed as $65,000.00 / $17

DMMS shares = 3823.50 sh

Cash after = $100,000.00 - $65,000.00

$$\boxed{\text{Cash after} = \$35,000.00}$$

We do the same for the Buy-and-Hold Portfolio. Note, 100% of the cash of the buy-and-hold portfolio must be used in buying the fund shares at $17. We're giving this portfolio an advantage which should be exclusive to the DMMS portfolio, to buy shares at the discounted price according to the DMMS Safety Factor Rule. So we compute the number of its shares as follows: $100,000.00 / $17

$$\boxed{\text{Buy-and-Hold shares} = 5882.35 \text{ sh.}}$$

At this time, the return (%) of both portfolios is 0%. We wait until the next move in the market, then we evaluate the two portfolios accordingly. Note, we don't know what we will do next; we'll let the market tell us what to do. Plugging all this information into our starting table, the table would look like this:

Table 10.1 Starting Table

STARTING INFORMATION FOR DMMS AND B&H INVESTORS			
Index	market index	Starting Date	Time unit 8
Index Fund	Index Fund	Starting Price = $17	
Starting Portfolio	$100,000		

DMMS STARTING INFORMATION	
Peak	$30
Safety Factor	30% initial drop, (Gridline 0%) Neutral Line
Risk Factor	35% of starting portfolio remains in cash
Cash	$35,000.00
Shares	$65,000.00 / $17 = 3823.50 sh
Shares Value	$65,000.00

B&H STARTING INFORMATION	
B&H Shares	$100,000.00 / $17 = 5882.35 sh
Shares Value	$100,000.00

After starting a DMMS position, the question becomes, what do we do next? By now, I am sure you know the answer to this question. We don't try to predict or outsmart the market, as most market participants do. No logical, or illogical, reason can be a good reason to try to bet on the next move in the market. We simply wait and let the market tell us what to do next.

But what do specifically wait for? We wait for a considerable move which causes the price to cross at least one gridline up or down. Otherwise, we do nothing, we just keep waiting until that happens. Can you see how much it's easier to not speculate and form useless opinions? Being right or wrong is irrelevant for a DMMS investor. If the price crosses a gridline down, we buy; if it crosses a gridline up, we sell. We'll buy or sell according to the DMMS rules.

Next time, unit 9 shows that price went from $17 to $25 crossing two gridlines: Gridline 0% and Gridline +10%. We always compare the current price to the previous price to decide what to do. Since the first gridline is below the Neutral Line, we sell only 5% of our shares. The second gridline is above the Neutral Line, we sell 10%. Therefore, we sell (5% + 10%) a total of 15% of our shares at $25 per share. We record our Cash Before and our Shares Before ahead of any market order. In this case, we have $35,000.00 in Cash and, 3823.50 shares. We do our transaction 15% (3823.50) = 573.5 sh to find out how many shares we need to sell. Then we execute our sell order 573.5 sh ($25) = $14337.50. At this point, we need to update our Cash After and our Shares After respectively.

Cash After = $35,000.00 + $14337.50 = $49337.50

Shares After = 3823.50 sh –573.50 sh = 3250 sh

In order to evaluate our DMMS Portfolio, we need to add the cash in the portfolio and the Shares Value.

Shares Value = 3250 sh ($25) = $81,250.00

DMMS Portfolio Value = $81,250.00 + $49337.50

= $130,587.50

Then we evaluate B&H Portfolio at $25.

5882.35 sh ($25) = $147,058.82

Now we can compute the Return % of both portfolios.

DMMS Portfolio Return =

(($130,587.50 – $100,000.00) / $100,000.00) 100%

DMMS Portfolio Return = 30.60%

Similarly, we compute the B&H Portfolio Return

(($147,058.82 – $100,000.00)/$100,000.00) 100%

B&H Portfolio Return = 47.06%

We are done with the evaluation for this time. Then we would wait again until the market tells us what to do next. During Time Unit 10, the market drops as reflected by the shares price declines from $25 to $20 crossing Gridline 0%. Since this decline is above the Neutral Line, we would buy shares only for 5% of our cash. We again update our Cash Before and our Shares Before, respectively.

Cash Before = $49,337.50

Shares Before = 3250 sh

Our transaction = 5% ($49,337.50) = $6,529.40

Now we execute our Buy Order

$6,529.40 / $20 = 326.50 sh

At this point, we must update our Cash After and our Shares After, respectively.

Cash After = $49,337.50 − $6,529.40 = $42,808.10

Shares After = 3250 sh + 326.50 sh = 3576.50 sh

Again we evaluate our DMMS Portfolio by adding our Cash After to Shares Value

Share Value = 3576.50 sh ($20) = $71,529.40

DMMS Portfolio Value = $42,808.10 + $71,529.40

= $114,337.50

Similarly, we evaluate the B&H Portfolio at $20

B&H Portfolio Value = 5882.35 sh ($20)

= $117,647.05

Now we compute the return of both portfolios the same way we did previously.

DMMS Portfolio Return =

(($114,337.50 – $100,000.00) / $100,000.00) 100%

DMMS Portfolio Return = 14.34%

Similarly, we compute the B&H Portfolio Return

(($117,647.05 – $100,000.00)/$100,000.00) 100%

B&H Portfolio Return = 17.65%

These calculations are very easy to do as it has been shown in Time units, 8,9, and 10. There is no reason for me to continue this detailed process as it becomes very obvious, clear, and redundant. A simple calculator, a spreadsheet formulation, or a computer program can further simplify this tedious process. I have included all the calculations for the 50-time units detailed in tables so that can serve as a guide on how we reach the results of our test for this system. I could have used easily spreadsheet functions or a computer program to produce these numerical values faster. But I realized that would not be helpful for my readers not to see how these numbers were produced. Looking just at numbers without showing how we got them might be somewhat confusing. For this reason, I decided to show the detailed process for every transaction. I don't expect readers to go over every detail, but I do expect that would be helpful in resolving any questions or confusion that might come along with the results. These tables are shown on the next few pages.

Time Unit	Price	Market Action	Cash Before	Shares Before	Transaction	Buy Order	Shares After	Sell Order	Cash After	Shares Value	DMMS Portfolio Value	B & H Portfolio Value	DMMS Return	B & H Return
1	$28	Safety Factor	$100,000.00	0	N/A	N/A	0	N/A	$100,000.00	0	$100,000	N/A	N/A	N/A
2	$30	Safety Factor	$100,000.00	0	N/A	N/A	0	N/A	$100,000.00	0	$100,000	N/A	N/A	N/A
3	$24	wait for a drop ≥30% from	$100,000.00	0	N/A	N/A	0	N/A	$100,000.00	0	$100,000	N/A	N/A	N/A
4	$28	Peak $30	$100,000.00	0	N/A	N/A	0	N/A	$100,000.00	0	$100,000	N/A	N/A	N/A
5	$25	($21 or less)	$100,000.00	0	N/A	N/A	0	N/A	$100,000.00	0	$100,000	N/A	N/A	N/A
6	$25		$100,000.00	0	N/A	N/A	0	N/A	$100,000.00	0	$100,000	N/A	N/A	N/A
7	$24		$100,000.00	0	N/A	N/A	0	N/A	$100,000.00	0	$100,000	N/A	N/A	N/A
8	43.3% from Peak $30 $17	$30 to $17 Risk Factor = 0.35 $100,000 (0.35) = $35,000 cash Buy shares with $65,000	$100,000.00	0	$65,000 / $17 = 3823.50 sh	3823.50 sh	3823.50 sh	N/A	$100,000 - $65,000 = $35,000	3823.5 sh ($17) 65000 = $65,000	$65,000 + $35,000 = $100,000	$100,000/$17 = 5882.35 sh $100,000	0%	0%
9	$25	$17 to $25 crossing Gridlines 0% and +10% sell 5% below neutral line and 10% above neutral line	$35,000.00	3823.5 sh	(5% + 10%) 3823.5 sh = 573.5 sh	N/A	3823.5 sh - 573.5 sh = 3250 sh	573.5 sh ($25) = $14,337.50	$35,000 + $14337.50 = $49,337.50	3250 sh ($25) = $81,250	$81,250 + $49,337.50 = $130,587.50	5882.35 sh ($25 = $147,058.82	30.60%	47.06%
10	$20	$25 to $20 crossing Gridline 0% buy 5% above neutral line	$49,337.50	3250 sh	5% ($49,337.50) $6,529.40	$6,529.40 / $20 = 326.50 sh	3250 sh + 326.50 sh = 3576.50 sh	N/A	$49,337.50 - ($20) $6,529.40 = $42,808.10	3576.50 sh ($20) = $71,529.40	$71,529.40 + $42,808.10 = $114,337.50	5882.35 sh ($20 = $117,647.05	14.34%	17.65%
11	$24	$20 to $24 crossing Gridline +10% sell 10% above neutral line	$42,808.10	3576.50 sh	10% (3576.50 sh) 357.7 sh	N/A	3576.50 sh - 357.70 sh = 3,218.80 sh	357.70 sh ($24) = $8,584.80	$42,808.10 + $8,584.80 = $51,392.90	3,218.80 sh ($24) = $77,251.20	$77,251.20 + $51,392.90 = $128,644.1	5882.35 sh ($24 = $141,176.47	28.64%	41.18%
12	$11	$24 to $11 crossing 4 gridlines, one above neutral line and 3 under neutral line, buy 5% above neutral line, (3 x 10%) under neutral line	$51,392.90	3218.80 sh	5% + 10% + 10% + 10%) $51,392.90 = $17,987.52	$17,987.52 / $11 = 1635.20 sh	3218.80 sh + 1635.20 sh = 4854 sh	N/A	$51,392.90 - $17,987.52 = $33,405.38	4854 sh ($11) = $53,394	$53,394 + $33,405.38 = $86,799.38	5882.35 sh ($11 = $64,705.88	-13.20%	-35.29%
13	$17	$11 to $17 crossing 2 gridlines under neutral line. sell (2 x 5%) under neutral line	$33,405.38	4854 sh	(2 x 5%) 4854 sh 485.4 sh	N/A	4854 sh - 485.4 sh = 4,368.6 sh	485.4 sh ($17) = $8,251.80	$33,405.38 + $8,251.80 = $41,657.18	4,368.6 sh ($17) = $74,266.2	$74,266.2 + $41,657.18 = $115,923.38	5882.35 sh ($17 = $100,000	15.92%	0%
14	$18	$17 to $18 no crossing here. No market action	$41,657.18	4,368.6 sh	N/A	N/A	4,368.6 sh	N/A	$41,657.18	4,368.6 sh ($18) = $78,634.80	$78,634.80 + $41,657.18 = $120,291.98	5882.35 sh ($18 = $105,882.30	20.29%	5.88%

Time Unit	Price	Market Action	Cash Before	Shares Before	Transaction	Buy Order	Shares After	Sell Order	Cash After	Shares Value	DMMS Portfolio Value	B & H Portfolio Value	DMMS Return	B & H Return
15	$26	$18 to $26 crossing one gridlines above neutral line. Sell 10%	$41,657.18	4,368.6 sh	(5% + 10%)4,368.6 sh = 655.29 sh	N/A	4,368.6 sh - 655.29 sh = 3,713.31 sh	655.29 sh ($26) = $17,037.54	$41,657.18 + $17,037.54 = $58,694.72	3,713.31 sh ($26) = $96,546.06	$96,546.06 + $58,694.72 = $155,240.78	5882.35 sh ($26) = $152,941.10	55.24%	52.94%
16	$28	$26 to $28 crossing one gridlines above neutral line. Sell 10%	$58,694.72	3,713.31 sh	(10%) 3,713.31 sh = 371.33 sh	N/A	3,713.31 sh - 371.33 sh = 3,341.98 sh	371.33 sh ($28) = $10,397.24	$58,694.72 + $10,397.24 = $69,091.96	3,341.98 sh ($28) = $93,575.44	$93,575.44 + $69,091.96 = $162,667.4	5882.35 sh ($28) = $164,705.80	62.67%	64.70%
17	$15	$28 to $15 crossing 4 gridlines, two above neutral line and two under neutral line Buy (5% + 5% + 10% + 10%)	$69,091.96	3,341.98 sh	(5% + 5% + 10% + 10%) $69091.96 = $20,727.59	$20,727.59 / $15 = 1,381.84 sh	3,341.98 sh + 1,381.84 sh = 4,723.82 sh	N/A	$69,091.96 - $20,727.59 = $48,364.37	4,723.82 sh ($15) = $70,857.30	$70,857.30 + $48,364.37 = $119,221.67	5882.35 sh ($15) = $88,235.25	19.22%	-11.76%
18	$11	$15 to $11 crossing one gridlines bellow neutral line. Buy 10%	$48,364.37	4,723.82 sh	10% ($48,364.37) = $4,836.44	$4,836.44 / $11 = 439.68 sh	4,723.82 sh + 439.68 sh = 5,163.50 sh	N/A	$48,364.37 - $4,863.44 = $43,500.93	5,163.50 sh ($11) = $56,798.46	$56,798.46 + $43,500.93 = $100,299.39	5882.35 sh ($11) = $64,705.85	0.30%	-35.29%
19	$16	$11 to $16 crossing one gridlines bellow neutral line. Sell 5%	$43,500.93	5163.50 sh	5% (5163.50 sh) = 258.17 sh	N/A	5,163.50 sh - 258.17 sh = 4,905.33 sh	258.17 sh ($16) = $4,130.72	$43,500.93 + $4,130.80 = $47,631.73	4,905.33 sh ($16) = $78,485.20	$78,485.20 + $47,631.73 = $126,116.93	5882.35 sh ($16) = $94,117.6	26.12%	-5.89%
20	$10	$16 to $10 crossing 2 gridlines bellow neutral line. Buy (10% + 10%)	$47,631.73	4,905.33 sh	20% ($47631.73) = $9,526.35	9,526.35 / $10 = 952.64 sh	4,905.33 sh + 952.64 sh = 5,857.97 sh	N/A	$47,631.73 - $9,526.35 = $38,105.38	5,857.97 sh ($10) = $58,579.70	$58,579.70 + $38,105.38 = $96,685.08	5882.35 sh ($10) = $58,823.50	-3.31%	-41.18%
21	$13	$10 to $13 crossing one gridline bellow neutral line. sell 5%	$38,105.38	5,857.97 sh	5% (5,857.97 sh) = 292.90 sh	N/A	5,857.97 sh - 292.90 sh = 5,565.07 sh	292.90 sh ($13) = $3,807.70	$38,105.38 + $3,807.70 = $41,913.08	5,565.07 sh ($13) = $72,345.91	$72,345.91 + $41,913.08 = $114,258.99	5882.35 sh ($13) = $76,470.55	14.26%	-23.53%
22	$6	$13 to $6 crossing two gridlines bellow neutral line. Buy (10% + 10%)	$41,913.08	5,565.07 sh	(10% + 10%) $41913.08 = $8,382.62	$8,382.62/$6 = 1,397.10 sh	5,565.07 sh + 1,397.10 sh = 6,962.17 sh	N/A	$41,913.08 - $8,382.62 = $33,530.46	6,962.17 sh ($6) = $41,773.04	$41,773.04 + $33,530.46 = $75,303.50	5882.35 sh ($6) = $35,294.10	-24.70%	-64.71%
23	$15	$6 to $15 crossing 3 gridlines bellow neutral line. Sell (5% + 5% + 5%)	$33,530.46	6,962.17 sh	(5% + 5% + 5%) 6,962.17 sh = 1,044.33 sh	N/A	6,962.17 sh - 1,044.33 sh = 5,917.84 sh	1,044.33 sh ($15) = $15,664.89	$33,530.46 + $15,664.89 = $49,195.35	5,917.84 sh ($15) = $88,767.66	$88,767.66 + $49,195.35 = $137,963.01	5882.35 sh ($15) = $88,235.25	37.96%	-11.76%
24	$20	$15 to $20 crossing two gridlines bellow neutral line. Sell (5% + 5%)	$49,195.35	5,917.84 sh	(5% + 5%) 5,917.84 sh = 591.78 sh	N/A	5,917.84 sh - 591.78 sh = 5,326.06 sh	591.78 sh ($20) = $11,835.60	$49,195.35 + $11,835.60 = $61,030.95	5,326.06 sh ($20) = $106,521.28	$106,521.28 + $61,030.95 = $167,552.23	5882.35 sh ($20) = $117,647	67.55%	17.65%

Time Unit	Price	Market Action	Cash Before	Shares Before	Transaction	Buy Order	Shares After	Sell Order	Cash After	Shares Value	DMMS Portfolio Value	B & H Portfolio Value	DMMS Return	B & H Return
25	$15	$20 to $15 crossing two gridlines bellow neutral line. Buy (10% + 10%)	$61,030.95	5,326.06 sh	(10% + 10%)	$12,206.19 / 813.75 sh	5,326.06 sh + 813.75 sh = 6,139.81 sh	N/A	$61,030.95 − $12,206.19 = $48,824.76	6,139.81 sh ($15) = $92,097.21	$92,097.21 + $48,824.76 = $140,921.97	5,882.35 sh ($15) = $88,235.25	40.92%	−11.76%
26	$19	$15 to $19 crossing one gridline bellow neutral line. Sell 5%	$48,824.76	6,139.81 sh	(5%) 6,139.81 sh = 307 sh	N/A	6,139.81 sh − 307 sh = 5,832.81 sh	307 sh ($19) = $5,832.82	$48,824.76 − $5,832.82 = $42,991.94	5,832.81 sh ($19) = $110,823.57	$110,823.57 + $42,991.94 = $153,815.51	5,882.35 sh ($19) = $111,764.65	53.81%	11.76%
27	$11	$19 to $11 crossing 2 gridlines bellow neutral line. Buy (10% + 10%)	$42,991.94	5,832.81 sh	(10% + 10%) $42,991.94 / $8,598.39	$8,598.38 / 781.67 sh	5,832.81 sh + 781.67 sh = 6,614.49 sh	N/A	$42,991.94 − $8,598.39 = $34,393.55	6,614.49 sh ($11) = $72,759.38	$72,759.38 + $34,393.55 = $107,152.93	5,882.35 sh ($11) = $64,705.85	7.15%	−35.84%
28	$18	$11 to $18 crossing 2 gridlines bellow neutral line. Sell (5% + 5%)	$34,393.55	6,614.49 sh	(5% + 5%) 6,614.49 sh = 661.45 sh	N/A	6,614.49 sh − 661.45 sh = 5,953.04 sh	661.45 sh ($18) = $11,906.10	$34,393.55 + $11,906.10 = $46,299.65	5,953.04 sh ($18) = $107,154.71	$107,154.71 + $46,299.65 = $153,454.36	5,882.35 sh ($18) = $105,882.30	53.45%	5.88%
29	$21	$18 to $21 crossing one gridline bellow neutral line. Sell 5%	$46,299.65	5,953.04 sh	(5%) 5,953.04 sh = 297.65 sh	N/A	5,953.04 sh − 297.65 sh = 5,655.39 sh	297.65 sh ($21) = $6,250.69	$46,299.65 + $6,250.69 = $52,550.34	5,655.39 sh ($21) = $118,763.15	$118,763.15 + $52,550.34 = $171,313.49	5,882.35 sh ($21) = $123,529.35	71.31%	23.53%
30	$17	$21 to $17 crossing one gridline bellow neutral line. Buy 10%	$52,550.34	5,655.39 sh	(10%) $52,550.34 / $5,255.03	$5,255.03 / 309.12 sh	5,655.39 sh + 309.12 sh = 5,964.51 sh	N/A	$52,550.34 − $5,255.03 = $47,295.31	5,964.51 sh ($17) = $101,396.66	$101,396.66 + $47,295.31 = $148,691.97	5,882.35 sh ($17) = $100,000.00	48.69%	0%
31	$23	$17 to $23 crossing two gridlines, one bellow neutral line, another above neutral line.	$47,295.31	5,964.51 sh	5,964.51 sh = 894.68 sh	N/A	5,964.51 sh − 894.68 sh = 5,069.83 sh	894.68 sh ($23) = $20,577.56	$47,295.31 + $20,577.56 = $67,872.86	5,069.83 sh ($23) = $116,606.17	$116,606.17 + $67,872.86 = $184,478.73	5,882.35 sh ($23) = $135,294.05	84.48%	35.29%
32	$28	$23 to $28 crossing one gridline above neutral line. Sell 10%	$67,872.86	5,069.83 sh	(10%) 5,069.83 sh = 506.98 sh	N/A	5,069.83 sh − 506.98 sh = 4,562.85 sh	506.98 sh ($28) = $14,195.44	$67,872.86 + $14,195.44 = $82,068.31	4,562.85 sh ($28) = $127,759.90	$127,759.90 + $82,068.31 = $209,828.21	5,882.35 sh ($28) = $164,705.80	109.83%	64.71%
33	$18	$28 to $18 crossing 3 gridlines, 2 above neutral line, and one bellow neutral line. Buy (5% + 5% + 10%)	$82,068.31	4,562.85 sh	(5% + 5% + 10%) $82,068.31 / $16,413.66	$16,413.66 / 911.87 sh	4,562.85 sh + 911.87 sh = 5,474.72 sh	N/A	$82,068.31 − $16,413.66 = $65,654.65	5,474.72 sh ($18) = $98,544.96	$98,544.96 + $65,654.65 = $164,199.61	5,882.35 sh ($18) = $105,882.30	64.20%	5.88%
34	$25	$18 to $25 crossing 2 gridlines, one above neutral line, another bellow neutral line. Sell (5% + 10%)	$65,654.65	5,474.72 sh	(5% + 10%) 5,474.72 sh = 821.21 sh	N/A	5,474.72 sh − 821.21 sh = 4,653.51 sh	821.21 sh ($25) = $20,530.20	$20,530.20 + $65,654.65 = $86,184.85	4,653.51 sh ($25) = $116,337.75	$116,337.75 + $86,184.85 = $202,522.60	5,882.35 sh ($25) = $147,058.75	102.52%	47.06%

Time Unit	Price	Market Action	Cash Before	Shares Before	Transaction	Buy Order	Shares After	Sell Order	Cash After	Shares Value	DMMS Portfolio Value	B&H Portfolio Value	DMMS Return	B&H Return
35	$26	$25 to $26 no crossing.	$86,184.85	4,653.51 sh	N/A	N/A	4,653.51 sh	N/A	$86,184.85	4,653.51 sh ($26) = $120,991.26	$207,176.11	5,882.35 sh ($26) = $152,941.10	107.18%	52.94%
36	$29	$26 to $29 crossing one gridline above neutral line. Sell 10%	$86,184.85	4,653.51 sh	4,653.51 sh (10%) = 465.35 sh	N/A	4,653.51 sh - 465.35 sh = 4,188.16 sh	465.35 sh ($29) = $13,495.15	$86,184.85 + $13,495.15 = $99,680	4,188.16 sh ($29) = $121,456.64	$221,136.64	5,882.35 sh ($29) = $170,588.15	121.14%	70.59%
37	$36	$29 to $36 crossing 2 gridlines above neutral line. Sell (10% + 10%)	$99,680.00	4,188.16 sh	(10% + 10%) 4,188.16 sh = 837.63 sh	N/A	4,188.16 sh - 837.63 sh = 3,350.53 sh	837.63 sh ($36) = $30,154.75	$99,680 + $30,154.75 = $129,834.75	3,350.53 sh ($36) = $120,619.01	$250,453.76	5,882.35 sh ($36) = $211,764.60	150.45%	111.76%
38	$27	$36 to $27 crossing 3 gridlines above neutral line. Buy (5% + 5% + 5%)	$129,834.75	3,350.53 sh	(5% + 5% + 5%) $129,834.75 = $19,475.21	$19,475.21 / ($27) = 721.30 sh	721.30 sh + 3,350.53 sh = 4,071.83 sh	N/A	$129,834.75 - $19,475.21 = $110,359.54	4,071.83 sh ($27) = $109,939.52	$220,479.06	5,882.35 sh ($27) = $158,823.45	110.48%	58.82%
39	$23	$27 to $23 crossing one gridline below neutral line. Buy 5%	$110,359.54	4,071.83 sh	$110,359.54 (5%) = $5,517.98	$5,517.98 / ($23) = 239.91 sh	239.91 sh + 4,071.83 sh = 4,311.74 sh	N/A	$110,359.54 - $5,517.98 = $104,841.56	4,311.74 sh ($23) = $99,170.12	$204,011.68	5,882.35 sh ($23) = $135,294.05	104.01%	35.29%
40	$26	$23 to $26 crossing one gridline above neutral line. Sell 10%	$104,841.56	4,311.74 sh	4,311.74 sh (10%) = 431.17 sh	N/A	4,311.74 sh - 431.17 sh = 3,880.57 sh	431.17 sh ($26) = $11,210.42	$104,841.56 + $11,210.42 = $116,051.98	3,880.57 sh ($26) = $100,894.93	$216,946.91	5,882.35 sh ($26) = $152,941.10	116.95%	52.94%
41	$14	$26 to $14 crossing 4 gridlines below new neutral line. Buy (10% + 10% + 10% + 10%)	$116,051.98	3,880.57 sh	(10% + 10% + 10% + 10%) $116,051.98 = $46,420.79	$46,420.79 / ($14) = 3,315.77 sh	3,315.77 sh + 3,880.57 sh = 7,196.34 sh	N/A	$116,051.98 - $46,420.79 = $69,631.19	7,196.34 sh ($14) = $100,748.76	$170,379.95	5,882.35 sh ($14) = $82,352.9	70.38%	-17.65%
42	$21	$14 to $21 crossing 2 gridlines below new neutral line. Sell (5% + 5%)	$69,631.19	7,196.34 sh	(5% + 5%) 7,196.34 sh = 719.63 sh	N/A	7,196.34 sh - 719.63 sh = 6,476.71 sh	719.63 sh ($21) = $15,112.23	$69,631.19 + $15,112.23 = $84,743.42	6,476.71 sh ($21) = $136,010.91	$220,754.33	5,882.35 sh ($21) = $123,529.35	120.75%	23.53%
43	$17	$21 to $17 crossing one gridline below neutral line. Buy 10%	$84,743.42	6,476.71 sh	$84,743.42 = $8,474.34	$8,474.34 / ($17) = 498.49 sh	498.49 sh + 6,476.71 sh = 6,975.20 sh	N/A	$84,743.42 - $8,474.34 = $76,269.08	6,975.20 sh ($17) = $118,578.41	$194,847.49	5,882.35 sh ($17) = $100,000.00	94.85%	0%
44	$13	$17 to $13 crossing one gridline below neutral line. Buy 10%	$76,269.08	6,975.20 sh	$76269.08 = $7626.91	$7626.91 / ($13) = 586.69 sh	6,975.20 sh + 586.69 sh = 7,561.89 sh	N/A	$76,269.08 - $7626.91 = $68,642.17	7,561.89 sh ($13) = $98,304.51	$166,946.68	5,882.35 sh ($13) = $76,470.55	66.95%	-23.26%

Time Unit	Price	Market Action	Cash Before	Shares Before	Transaction	Buy Order	Shares After	Sell Order	Cash After	Shares Value	DMMS Portfolio Value	B & H Portfolio Value	DMMS Return	B & H Return
45	$12	$13 to $12 no crossing	$68,642.17	7,561.89 sh	N/A	N/A	7,561.89 sh	N/A	$68,642.17	7,561.89 sh ($12) = $90,742.62	$68,642.17 + $90,742.62 = $159,384.79	5,882.35 sh ($12) = $70,588.20	59.38%	-29.41%
46	$19	$12 to $19 crossing 2 gridlines bellow neutral line. Sell (5% + 5%)	$68,642.17	7,561.89 sh	(5% + 5%) 7,561.89 sh = 756.19 sh	N/A	7,561.89 sh - 756.19 sh = 6,805.70 sh	756.19 sh ($19) = $14,367.61	$68,642.17 + $14,367.61 = $83,009.78	6,805.70 sh ($19) = $129,308.21	$83,009.78 + $129,308.21 = $212,317.99	5,882.35 sh ($19) = $111,764.65	112.32%	11.76%
47	$20	$19 to $20 no crossing. No action	$83,009.78	6,805.70 sh	N/A	N/A	6,805.70 sh	N/A	$83,009.78	6,805.70 sh ($20) = $136,113.91	$83,009.78 + $136,113.91 = $219,123.69	5,882.35 sh ($20) = $117,647.00	119.12%	17.65%
48	$25	$20 to $25 crossing 2 gridlines bellow neutral line. Sell (5% + 5%)	$83,009.78	6,805.70 sh	(5% + 5%) 6,805.70 sh = 680.57 sh	N/A	6,805.70 sh - 680.57 sh = 6,125.13 sh	680.57 sh ($25) = $17,014.25	$17,014.25 + $83,009.78 = $100,024.03	6,125.13 sh ($25) = $153,128.13	$100,024.03 + $153,128.13 = $253,152.16	5,882.35 sh ($25) = $147,058.75	153.15%	47.06%
49	$26	$25 to $26 no crossing. No action	$100,024.03	6,125.13 sh	N/A	N/A	6,125.13 sh	N/A	$100,024.03	6,125.13 sh ($26) = $159,253.26	$100,024.03 + $159,253.26 = $259,277.29	5,882.35 sh ($26) = $152,941.10	159.28%	52.94%
50	$21	$26 to $21 crossing 2 gridlines bellow neutral line. Sell (5% + 5%)	$100,024.03	6,125.13 sh	(5% + 5%) 6,125.13 sh = 612.51 sh	N/A	6,125.13 sh - 612.51 sh = 5,512.62 sh	612.51 sh ($21) = $12,862.71	$100,024.03 + $12,862.71 = $112,886.74	5,512.62 sh ($21) = $115,764.92	$112,886.74 + $115,764.92 = $228,651.66	5,882.35 sh ($21) = $123,529.35	128.65%	23.53%

CHAPTER 11

DMMS EVALUATION

From the tables shown in the previous chapter, we can see DMMS Portfolio's return has improved continuously over time in up, down, and sideways market moves. Certainly, both DMMS and the Buy-and-Hold investors were wrong on the market direction in the beginning even after the initial drop since the market went lower later on. In this chapter, we are going to evaluate the performance of the two portfolios side by side in all market conditions, at the peak, at the bottom, and at the breaking-even point in time.

We can see from the data shown in the performance tables two important things to mention. When the price moved higher in Time Unit 9, from $17 to $25, the DMMS portfolio underperformed the B & H portfolio initially. This is to be expected in the beginning when the market moves higher, since the B & H portfolio owns more shares than the DMMS portfolio. However, as time goes by, the DMMS will catch up and outperform the B & H even on the upside considerably. Notice, this is the only time the DMMS portfolio underperforms the B & H portfolio. On the other hand, when the market declined in Time Unit 12 to $11, the DMMS was outperforming the B & H by 22%. This is also to be expected in the beginning since the B & H owns more shares and the loss would be greater. These results are not surprising at all, just as expected at the start of a new trade using this system.

Nonetheless, as time goes by, and the market fluctuates, the DMMS portfolio's performance takes off and continues to outperform in all market conditions. This outperformance is fueled by the fluctuations of the market in bull and bear territories alike. Unlike most market participants who gamble on market direction and get whipsawed, DMMS never gets whipsawed by market fluctuations. The system does not speculate, it simply follows the market instead of trying to lead it as most people do, trying to impose their opinions on the market. From the results shown in our data, we can see that DMMS has turned the market into a business of buying shares at lower prices and selling these accumulated shares at much higher prices. Also, unlike the B & H portfolio which is fully invested all the time, the DMMS portfolio would be collecting some earned interest on its cash portion in its portfolio. As I mentioned previously, I avoided showing that accrued interest part in our data just for the sake of simplification. The financial company of the index fund would compute this interest to the DMMS portfolio automatically.

Furthermore, as we continue this evaluation of these two portfolios, we can see that the index fund share value reached a bottom during Time Unit 22 of $6. That is quite a decline from the recent peak of $30 in Time Unit 2 before starting this trade. We can see now that both portfolios were wrong in the direction of the market. Nevertheless, while DMMS was at a loss of -24.70%, the B & H hold was at a whopping loss of -64.71%. The market drop from $30 to $6 was -80.0% from the original peak. The B & H lost only -64.71% instead of -80.0%, thanks to the Safety Factor, we allowed this portfolio to take advantage of it. Notice the DMMS portfolio lost only -24.70% relative to the market loss of -80.0% and -64.71% of the B & H. The DMMS outperformed the market by 55.3% and the B & H by 40.0%. That is a remarkable performance during a very severe bear market.

As time goes by, days, weeks, or months, whatever we wish to consider this time horizon, we can see that DMMS performance always kept increasing in all market conditions. When the market reached a new all-time high price, as a new peak at $36 in Time Unit 37. Notice that the DMMS Return reached 150.45% while the B & H was up by 111.76%. The DMMS outperformed the B & H even at the all-time high new peak by 39%. Even the B & H was fully invested from the beginning, the DMMS outperformed.

Finally, as we move to the end of the testing data, Time Unit 50, we can see that the price of those shares declined to $21. We can see that the B & H portfolio is still up by +23.53% thanks to allowing it to take advantage of the Safety Factor. Nonetheless, the DMMS reached a gain of 128.65%, beating the B & H by 105%. While the market was -30.00% at $21, the DMMS was beating the market by 158.65%. Now, this is a remarkable result in my opinion when we are talking about a whole portfolio in comparison to the market. Remember, 75 to 85% of money managers underperform the market every year. In my humble opinion, I find the performance of the system quite impressive. I am not really surprised by these results, because DMMS strives on the fluctuations of the market. All markets fluctuate one way or another, both in bear and bull markets. That's why the DMMS will always outperform the market, and certainly the buy-and-hold, in the long run in all market conditions.

While our test data are not originated from real market data, because I did not want to use any particular name in this test, also for a simpler illustration of the system. But I do agree, the market rarely makes large moves in a short time. So the time units of days might not be realistic at all, but the weekly or monthly periods are more reasonable. Also, in a real market, time periods are not equal; they can be short and long. Of course, some of these moves are exaggerated for the purpose of demonstrating the concept step by step. Nonetheless, we know that every market fluctuates, regardless if that happens slowly or quickly with different intensities. The bottom line is, this system strives on these fluctuations. Since all markets fluctuate, the system will always outperform in the long run. I am including in the following pages some of the performance tables and charts for your review.

Time Unit	Price	DMMS Return	B & H Return	Performance
1	$28	0	0	0%
2	$30	0	0	0%
3	$24	0	0	0%
4	$25	0	0	0%
5	$28	0	0	0%
6	$25	0	0	0%
7	$24	0	0	0%
8	43.3% from Peak $30 $17	0%	0%	0%
9	$25	30.60%	47.06%	-16%
10	$20	14.34%	17.65%	-3%
11	$24	28.64%	41.18%	-13%
12	$11	-13.20%	-35.29%	22%
13	$17	15.92%	0%	16%
14	$18	20.29%	5.88%	14%
15	$26	55.24%	52.94%	2%
16	$28	62.67%	64.70%	-2%
17	$15	19.22%	-11.76%	31%
18	$11	0.30%	-35.29%	36%
19	$16	26.12%	-5.89%	32%
20	$10	-3.31%	-41.18%	38%
21	$13	14.26%	-23.53%	38%
22	$6	-24.70%	-64.71%	40%
23	$15	37.96%	-11.76%	50%
24	$20	67.55%	17.65%	50%
25	$15	40.92%	-11.76%	53%

Time Unit	Price	DMMS Return	B & H Return	Performance
26	$19	53.81%	11.76%	42%
27	$11	7.15%	-35.84%	43%
28	$18	53.45%	5.88%	48%
29	$21	71.31%	23.53%	48%
30	$17	48.69%	0%	49%
31	$23	84.48%	35.29%	49%
32	$28	109.83%	64.71%	45%
33	$18	64.20%	5.88%	58%
34	$25	102.52%	47.06%	55%
35	$26	107.18%	52.94%	54%
36	$29	121.14%	70.59%	51%
37	$36	150.45%	111.76%	39%
38	$27	110.48%	58.82%	52%
39	$23	104.01%	35.29%	69%
40	$26	116.95%	52.94%	64%
41	$14	70.38%	-17.65%	88%
42	$21	120.75%	23.53%	97%
43	$17	94.85%	0%	95%
44	$13	66.95%	-23.26%	90%
45	$12	59.38%	-29.41%	89%
46	$19	112.32%	11.76%	101%
47	$20	119.12%	17.65%	101%
48	$25	153.15%	47.06%	106%
49	$26	159.25%	52.29%	107%
50	$21	128.65%	23.53%	105%

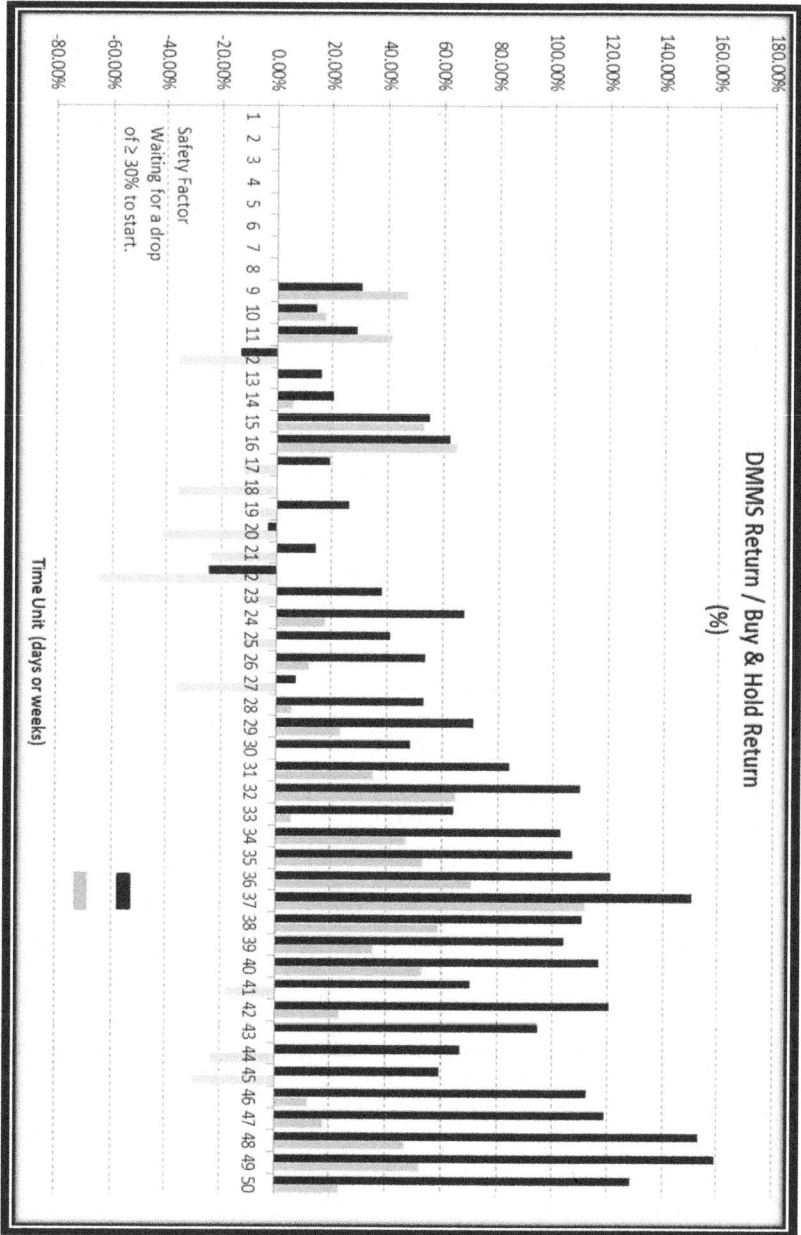

DMMS Return / Buy & Hold Return (%)

Time Unit (days or weeks)

Safety Factor
Waiting for a drop
of ≥ 30% to start.

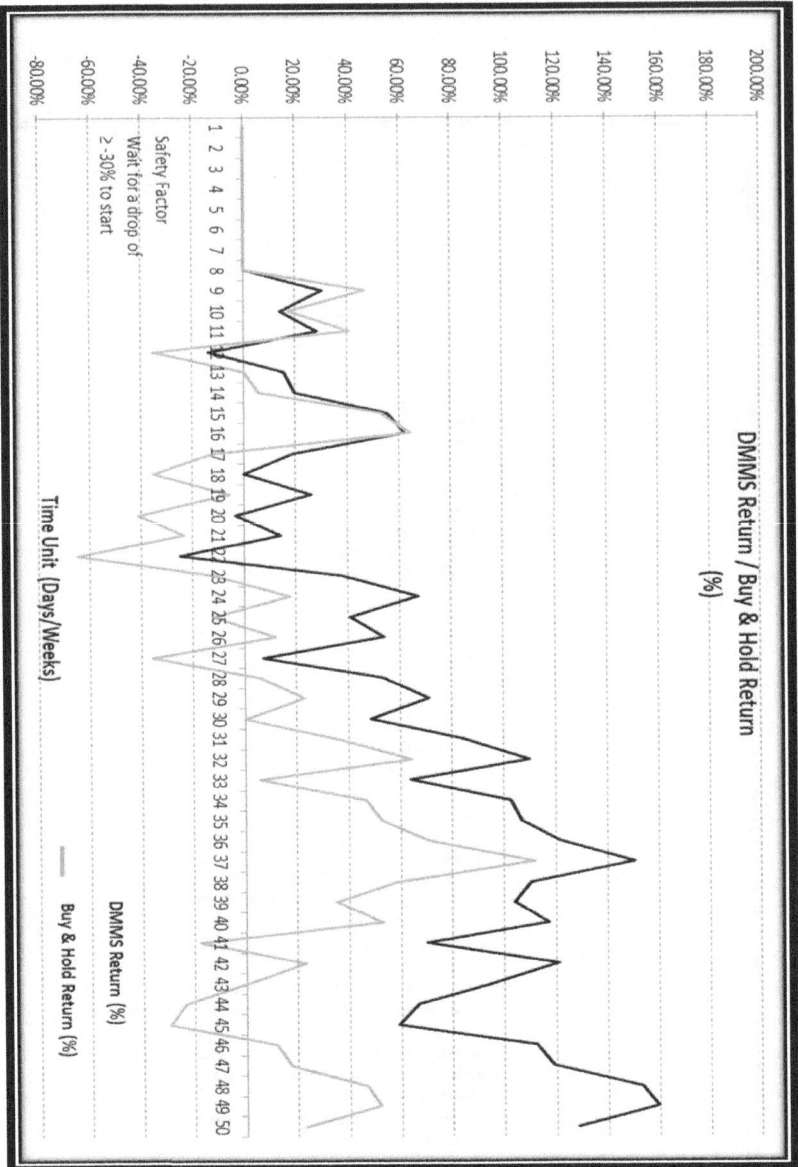

DMMS Return / Buy & Hold Return
(%)

Safety Factor
Wait for a drop of
≥ -30% to start

Time Unit (Days/Weeks)

DMMS Return (%)

Buy & Hold Return (%)

Often, market participants try to reduce their risk by using "loss stops". As the name implies; it's a loss stop. That means the investor is incurring a loss every time that stop is hit. That's the main reason why most traders lose money, as they try to limit their losses when they speculate on market direction. Fortunately, this is what the DMMS avoids entirely, and uses these fluctuations to accumulate more gains with time. If you are an investor who happened to be a buy-and-hold investor, and you experienced the crash of 1929 or the crash of dot.com, you would be waiting miserably a few decades just to break even assuming you are invested in the general market, not in individual stocks. On the other hand, a DMMS investor can weather these horrible bear markets quite nicely by using these natural fluctuations to strive and show considerable gains during such a miserable time.

The most amazing part of this outstanding performance is the fact that we did not need to be right on the market. In fact, we were wrong! Yet, it did not matter; we did not need to predict anything. In real market involvement, we would not lose our night's sleep because of fear and anxiety worrying about the future of our investments, as would be the case for buy-and-hold investors. They would be very lucky in the end if they can break even if they go through a severe bear market. As DMMS investors, all we need is a market that continues to exist and does what a market usually does, that is, to fluctuate up and down. Imagine how simple our investing style would be when all we have to think about is one or two markets, instead of worrying about thousands of individual stocks and thousands of actively managed mutual funds lost in an ocean of confusion and madness.

The secret of the DMMS's outstanding performance is not a secret at all. Simply said, no need to try to outsmart the market; just let the market tell you what to do. Outsmarting the market is nothing more than our human arrogance trying to impose our opinions on the market and expecting it to do what we want, wish, or expect it to do. Following popular technical and fundamental analyses used by everyone else is way overrated. I said previously, and I repeat myself here: if you can see it, so does everyone else. Therefore, it's already discounted by the market. If you know what everyone else knows, you know nothing of real value. Trends do sometimes exist in the market, but we can never tell how long the trend can last and when it will reverse. Thus, what we see is what already happened. Unfortunately, many people think this is what is about to happen.

If drawing lines and studying chart patterns can tell us where the market is going, everyone would become a technician and everyone would become rich. But we know that is not true at all. It is so irritating and misleading when we hear some people swear by these trendlines, moving averages, resistances, or supports that they can tell you how the market would move next. They tell us arrogantly where the market would go, in a direction they can foresee. The problem with that is, at any point in time and price, the odds are not better or worse than 50%. What does that mean? That is nothing short of gambling in the greatest casino in the world. But this is not just a game of fun and entertainment; it's gambling with your hard-earned money and your life sweat.

Traders are often fooled by those "loss stops". But after getting whipsawed many times by market fluctuations, they realize sooner than later that such stops are just giving away their money gradually. These stops steer the market in their direction, and they get hit. Then the market reverses in the opposite direction and hit those stops too. That's why the market keeps fluctuating up and down during the trading day for no other reasons, besides going after these stops. This is not a secret at all. The market is a jungle where everyone is waiting to feed on the others, and that is no exaggeration. Masses are drawn to it by greed until fear disappears. History repeats itself, in every market, over and over. Investing becomes speculation; another socially accepted way of describing gambling. However, investing using DMMS is another way of using these fluctuations to its advantage and turning the market into a business of buying and selling shares instead of a casino.

How is DMMS different from everything out there? Well, everything you read or hear requires you to choose a direction hoping that you and your advisor are correct on your bet, whether it's a fund, an individual stock, an option, or even the general market. If you are wrong, you would lose some or all your invested money, and you still have to pay the cost of that advice for that recommendation. Furthermore, every technical and fundamental indicator becomes obsolete with time as market participants become aware of its effects and act earlier and earlier.

Well, one might be tempted at this point to wonder if the same thing can be applied to DMMS. Fortunately not! Think about it, for a system to become obsolete, it must use a particular signal or indicator to give a clue about where the market is heading. When enough people start doing the same thing ahead of each other, trying to catch the advantage earlier and earlier, the system loses its predictive effectiveness and fades away with time. The reason is every system out there requires you to take a position on the market by choosing a direction hoping the market would move your way. DMMS, on the other hand, does not require you to choose a direction. It's even irrelevant if you are right or wrong. In fact, we were wrong in our test on the market direction. Furthermore, we know that the market will always fluctuate, and we know that DMMS always strives for these fluctuations.

We saw from the test results shown previously, that the DMMS continues to outperform the buy-and-hold in all market environments. This outperformance continues to increase as time goes by, regardless of whether the market goes up, down, or sideways; it's really irrelevant in the long run. As long as the market continues to exist and continues to move, the DMMS continues to strive. DMMS will never become obsolete, even if every investor would use it. That would actually increase the volatility in the market, which is the best of all worlds for this system. In other words, you don't need the market to go higher to make money, all you need is a market that keeps "breathing" and fluctuating up and down even if it goes nowhere.

I am dedicating my next and final chapter of this book to answering commonly asked questions about DMMS. I am now about to conclude my work in this book showing why traditional investing does not always work; why no one can predict market moves; how the first spark led me to create DMMS; how the digital concept can be applied to the market as well as in electronics in the real world; and how to eliminate the need for guessing when you use this approach in dealing with the market.

Most likely, if you are in the market, you consider yourself an investor or at most a trader, but most likely not a gambler. Otherwise, you would find yourself in a more pleasant casino with attractive people trying to serve you and make your stay pleasant and entertaining. Your dollar certainly would stretch more in a casino, buying you all the thrill you want. However, I assume you are in the market to make money. Market entertainment is very costly and less entertaining. The problem is you have been taught to invest like everyone else, then you wonder what else you did not do to not show better results. The market simply never allows the majority to win for a long time. It's such an ironic paradox. The market requires a free democratic system to survive and flourish; yet, the market itself is anything but a democracy. The market is almost always on the side of the minority. Then, in order to survive in the market, you must move from being on the majority side to the minority side. Most likely you heard "it's a game with a sum equals zero". The dollar one makes is the dollar someone else or many more else lose.

Buying and holding in a long-running bull market is a wonderful thing, assuming that the bull can keep running endlessly. But we know, sooner or later, a bear will catch up with the bull, and all that gain over the years will evaporate if you are lucky enough you caught the bull run early enough. However, if you are one of those unlucky ones who caught the bull at the end of its run, you will end up with great losses that may take years if ever to recover. DMMS takes advantage of such a reality and capitalizes on bull and bear phases during a market cycle. This explains the great performance of DMMS even in a poor market. Certainly, if you can do well in a poor market, there is no reason to do any worse in a good market. Unlike the unrealistic wish of the buy-and-hold investor for a long, never-ending bull market, the DMMS investor is more realistic and accepts the natural occurrence of market cycles.

A bear market simply is not any better or worse than a bull market in terms of this investing system. Both phases of the market cycle are needed to create a more balanced market that reflects the natural order of supply and demand. Both markets provide different opportunities as well. The bear phase provides the opportunity to load on shares at discounted prices. The bull phase, on the other hand, provides the opportunity to unload these shares at premium prices.

It's not the bear market that really hurts; it's the lack of cash in a bear market that does hurt. We may think as well that earthquakes hurt, while in reality, only falling objects do. DMMS can become an important tool in your investing world and can be a very effective tool. However, if you like to speculate, you are just gambling, and maybe you are better off doing that in a casino. You certainly need more good luck in gambling than in investing using DMMS. Therefore, I wish you the best of both of these worlds.

CHAPTER 12

FREQUENTLY ASKED QUESTIONS

I am concluding my work in this book with this final chapter addressing every question I have been asked or any possible question that I can think of that might be helpful to my readers. I am starting first with the most obvious and simple question that most people ask me.

Question 1. Do you personally use DMMS in investing your portfolio?

Answer: Yes, I apply everything I said and explained in this book to my own portfolio. In fact, this is the only way I feel comfortable enough investing at a portfolio level in the market. I have been trading the financial markets for about 29 years. I have traded every investment instrument that moves up and down, starting with individual stocks, mutual funds, commodities, options on commodities and stocks, etc. You name it, and most likely I traded it. However, this is the only way I invest at a portfolio level, the DMMS way. I never speculate on the market direction.

Question 2. What indices do you use with DMMS?

Answer: I personally prefer using the general market index for the obvious reason of safety and diversification. I share my opinion and my personal experience with my readers, but nothing should be considered a recommendation. I especially like to use the SP500 and the NASDAQ. These two indices fit very well my investment objective. I am very pleased with the result of using DMMS for all these years. Think about it! How many fund managers can beat the market year after year and by how much? We already know 75 to 85% of them underperform the market every year.

Question 3. Do you always wait for an initial large drop in an index to start a DMMS position?

Answer: Yes, absolutely, and the larger the initial drop the better it is. As you know, Safety Factor is a very important rule in DMMS. It should be at least between 25 to 35% from the peak. I know that does not happen very often, but it's worth it to wait for its occurrence. Often we are tempted to jump immediately on a market that has been moving up for a long time. Buying near the market peak is the most detrimental to a portfolio when the market reverses and drops much faster to the downside. Specialized sectors in the market can be more dramatic when they decline. Patience would pay off in time; no need to approach the market emotionally. This is the whole purpose of DMMS, to avoid speculation and not to make financial decisions based only on opinions and emotions.

Question 4. Do you prefer to use time or price to evaluate periodically your DMMS portfolio?

Answer: I personally prefer using price as a basis for a market action or no action. Both ways, price and time, have some advantages and disadvantages. For example, when the market moves up or down by 10 to 20% in a relatively short time, I like to take advantage of this unusual volatility. The market sometimes moves back and forth several times before making up its mind and moving in one direction. These fluctuations are enormously beneficial for DMMS. We can buy and sell shares during this volatile time, even when the market is going nowhere. DMMS strives on fluctuations more than on trends. During this time, the buy-and-hold investor would be getting frustrated and making no gain at all.

Similarly, using time as the basis instead of price in evaluating DMMS has its own advantages and disadvantages. You might want to do that on a weekly, monthly, or quarterly basis. The advantage of that is, the current price relative to the price of the previous evaluation might be much lower or much higher, giving you a great opportunity to buy or sell at a great price. Another advantage would be you don't need to monitor the market very often, as is the case when you're using price as your basis. On the other hand, the disadvantage of using time instead of price as your basis is that sometimes the market might make several moves in both directions between your evaluation time. Furthermore, the market might return to where it was during the previous evaluation, depriving you of any market action.

So which basis is best, price or time? The choice is yours. If you are too busy in your daily life, and you have no time to monitor the market often, the time basis would be better for you. On the other hand, if you were actively involved in the market, the price basis would be the best choice. This is, as I said previously, my personal choice. I would like to take advantage of these fluctuations as often as it's possible.

Question 5: Is DMMS' way of investing similar to the popular dollar cost-averaging method that most mutual funds advise their shareholders?

Answer: Absolutely not, how so? Dollar-cost averaging implies that an investor buys shares periodically with a fixed small amount of money regardless of what the market does, resulting in more shares bought on the downside and fewer shares bought on the upside. While this is not something I would do, that is certainly much better than not investing at all. This has been a very popular approach by mutual funds firms to encourage millions of employees in most corporations to participate in the market and invest their retirement funds, IRAs, and 401Ks periodically and automatically. Actually, this is the bloodline of the financial market for some time. Mutual funds usually discourage investors from trading or timing the market. To do so, the fund performance is affected when the fund is forced to sell shares to redeem some shareholders, especially during volatile times.

Furthermore, dollar cost averaging does not require investors to sell at any time or change the degree of aggressiveness toward the market. An employee with a limited income can contribute a small amount periodically and steadily over time, drawn directly from his employment earning. I would certainly prefer dollar cost averaging over the buy-and-hold way of investing. Dollar-cost averaging gives the investor the opportunity to participate in all market conditions without getting whipsawed. Dollar-cost averaging is basically a passive way of investing for small investors with limited income, time, and knowledge of investment. Furthermore, the dollar-cost-averaging investor does not sell those accumulated shares at different times, and often it's used in the company's stock. That is an unacceptable risk in my opinion. Such an investor is very much like the buy-and-hold, investing in increments instead of a lump sum.

However, if the investor is sitting on a considerably large amount of cash, dollar cost averaging is an extremely poor way to invest since it cannot be efficiently useful in dealing with lump sum investments. As shown previously in this book, DMMS investing involves buying and selling with varying degrees of aggressiveness relative to price movements. Also, DMMS buys and sells at any time and enjoys the benefits of volatile markets. In DMMS, a market direction is irrelevant, and this type of investor is actively participating in the market without speculating on a particular outcome.

Question 6: Is not buying on the downside and selling on the upside just another way of buying on weakness and selling on strength?

Answer: Personally, I think it's a great mistake to accumulate more shares in an individual stock or an actively managed fund on weakness. An individual stock may go up to the sky, then tumbles back to earth and ceases to exist. Your money would evaporate regardless of the number of shares you own of that stock. Similarly, I don't feel much better about buying into a declining actively managed fund, while the market is advancing. That is strong proof that the fund is in serious trouble.

However, there is a major difference when we invest using DMMS; we are investing only in the general market indices and only after an initial decline determined by the Safety Factor around 35% from the peak. Buying the market on weakness after a steep decline and selling it on strength after a strong advance is different from dealing with an individual stock or a fund. While the stock market is not a physical commodity like most commodities, the stock market is a financial commodity, and the natural law of supply and demand still has considerable influence on this financial commodity.

Like most commodities, the law of supply and demand sometimes is disturbed by manipulative powerful groups or governments. Crude oil, for example, is manipulated by OPEC; gold is manipulated by central banks around the world; and the stock market is manipulated by the Federal Reserve. When the market advances too fast, the Fed tries to talk it down, either by comments or by raising the interest rate.

A good example of that is the "exuberance" comment by Chairman Greenspan years ago. When the market drops sharply, like the crash in 1987 or September 11, 2001, the Fed comes to the rescue by commenting or cutting the interest rate sharply. So for this reason, it is justified in my opinion to consider buying in weakness since it represents a great value. Similarly, selling as the market advances strongly in a short time causes the market to be overvalued. This is an opportunity in my opinion to sell those shares at premium prices. This is exactly what we mean by buying low and selling high.

As shown, the market does not keep going up forever, nor does it keep going down forever as well, certainly not to zero or near that. Either way, it goes, it does not get there in a straight line. Therefore, supply and demand set the appropriate market value. I see a justified reason to sell in an advancing market taking profit and to buy in a declining market, accumulating more shares at bargain prices. DMMS provides this mechanism in a systematic approach without the need to speculate on the market or to try to time it.

Question 7: Contrary to most gurus and money managers out there, why doesn't DMMS investing emphasize the use of fundamental and technical analyses?

Answer: I know many market participants and professional money managers use fundamental and technical analyses. While these analyses can tell you everything about the past, they tell you nothing about the future. It's a great way to look at the past and try to form opinions and speculate on future market moves. In my opinion, they don't have any foresight into the future whatsoever. Everything you see or hear, most likely the majority of market participants know about it as well. As I said previously throughout this book, if you know what everyone else knows, you know nothing that would help you know what the market will do. Simply, this information is already well discounted by the market and reflected in the price.

Even knowing what other people don't know would not help much. Are you surprised? Why do I say that? Because market participants don't react the same way to the same news, regardless of whether the news is good or bad. Some people sell on good news, thinking it's a good opportunity to unload their shares, driving prices lower instead of higher. Similarly, some people buy on bad news, thinking it's a good opportunity to load on shares, driving prices higher. That would throw off all logic behind this approach.

Although I have a strong technical background, I have a very difficult time accepting that a particular chart, pattern, or line on the chart has as much predictive power as some people want to believe. If you see it, then others see it too. Therefore, it's worthless in terms of predictive power of future market moves. Otherwise, you would see people flocking to school to learn about these "tricks" and everyone would become rich. But we know that is not true at all from what we see in reality. Many highly educated people with PhDs in economics and the financial field spend their lives going nowhere beyond their comfortable teaching jobs.

In addition to what these analyses can tell me about the past, I find them very useful in telling me what other market participants might be thinking and what they might do or not do. But the question always remains the same: "what would the market do next?" No one can answer this question accurately, besides presenting an opinion and speculating on market direction. Since the market has the tendency to go to an equilibrium state at any moment in time, there is no way for anyone to predict what the market would do next accurately without speculation.

Question 8: Outperforming the market and the buy-and-hold in a sideways or declining market is an obvious feature of DMMS. Does the system also outperform in a strong advancing market?

Answer: The answer is yes and no. No, in the very short term, assuming the market will immediately advance without any retreat or fluctuations. In this case, the cash amount determined by the Risk Factor of 35% would be a drag on the total DMMS portfolio. The answer is yes, as we saw in our testing, the DMMS catches up in a relatively short time and does not look back anymore even in an advancing market. After all, even an advancing market fluctuates from time to time, right? That would certainly contribute to the DMMS gain even in an advancing market. Definitely, the DMMS should always outperform in the long and intermediate terms in any market conditions, as has been shown by our testing results.

Realistically, a market never goes up or down in a straight line for a long time. As the market advances sharply, a considerable number of traders become nervous and start to jump off the wagon. They start selling because they want to lock in those gains, causing the market to decline. When such declines occur, DMMS triggers more buying opportunities. Remember, the price reference at the neutral line would adapt to the new advancements in the market as a new peak is reached. The neutral line moves higher and higher as the market keeps advancing to new peaks, establishing a new neutral line at 65% of the new peak. This is a great feature that keeps DMMS in the market basically all the time, compounding profit. Hence, DMMS will always be outperforming the market and the buy-and-hold portfolio in all market conditions, up, down, or sideways in the long term.

Question 9: "The trend is your friend." Why does DMMS go against the trend by buying in a declining market and selling in an advancing market?

Answer: Stating that a market is "declining" or "advancing" in the progressive form implies a continuous motion in the same direction. There is a future element in such a statement that bothers me to assume that we know what is coming next based just on what happened in the past. To assume that a trend is going to continue is certainly a wrong and risky assumption. Otherwise, all we need to do is to find trends on the chart and ride them, and everyone would become rich. Reality is far from being that simple. Although, trends develop in the market, regardless of how short or long a particular trend might last, such a trend can reverse anytime without much of a warning.

At any moment in time, the market is in a state of equilibrium or trying to reach such a state when its equilibrium is disturbed. When the market is in a state of equilibrium, the odds are very close to 50%. Thus, it is almost impossible to tell what would the market do next based just on the past history. Betting on or against a trend is simply another way of sophisticated gambling. Trends may seem to be easy to trade. Nevertheless, by the time you recognize the trend, a great portion of that trend is already a part of that past history. Furthermore, if you stay long enough in it to find out when it would reverse, you would realize very often that you lost most of your previous gain, if any, or maybe you are already at a loss before you get out. Most of the time, trend traders are late going in and late as well getting out of the trade.

I know that may not sound very wise to buy in a declining market and to sell in an advancing market, since the decline or the advance may continue. However, remember in DMMS we assume that "we don't know" what the market would do next. We don't lead the market as most people do, we just follow the market. We don't predict the market direction; we know no one can. Only naive people think they can. Brokers and advisers think they can too for a different reason; they make their living from their opinions and recommendations.

After all, up or down is irrelevant in DMMS. Remember, we welcome both outcomes with no preference. We like to buy shares as much as we like to sell them. We always have some cash to buy with and some shares to sell. Furthermore, we buy and sell with some aggressiveness at the right time in all market conditions. Markets always fluctuate regardless if they are trending or not, and that is wonderful for DMMS.

Question 10: Since you are not a trend follower, do you still use charts?

Answer: Yes, of course, but in a different way than most people do.   Chart patterns don't have all that predictive power that we hear about. Nevertheless, people who are technically oriented would always find an explanation for every change on the chart. I simply use the chart to tell me where the market has been instead of where it is going. Supports and resistances, for example, are only the price levels where the struggle between bulls and bears becomes more intensified. One can never tell ahead of time whether the breakout would be to the upside or to the downside.

While a chart cannot tell you which direction the market will move next, it can tell you something about the past and the points of struggles between market forces.   Of course, the other use of the chart is to use it to apply the DMMS strategy and rules that we talked about in this book.

Question 11: Do you use options to hedge your DMMS position?

Answer: Options are not necessary to hedge a DMMS position, since we don't care if the market goes up or down; it's really irrelevant in this case. Some people use options to place a bet on an individual stock or a commodity or whatever, in one direction or another. This is precisely what I call gambling and pure speculation. I have no interest whatsoever in this kind of use of options. Options are advertised as limited-risk investments where a loss is limited to the premium one pays for the option's contract. Frankly, risking 100% of your total option premium is not a limited risk in my opinion at all.

But I would not mind using options as a part of DMMS when I want to buy shares or sell shares. These are covered options, that is, writing options contracts against my shares in the DMMS index fund. For example, I might want to buy some shares anyway at a particular price of the index. So I write a Put option contract for those shares and I receive the premium from the option buyer. In other words, someone is paying me to buy those shares at that price, which I am planning to buy them anyway. If the market declines to that price, I must buy those shares at that price and I keep that premium. Similarly, I can use the covered Call Option to write contracts to sell my shares at a higher price of my choice that I want to sell anyway. The option buyer would pay me the premium for me to keep. If the market reaches that high price, I have the obligation to sell those shares, which I was planning to sell anyway. This way, I generate more income from my shares by writing options contract in Puts and Calls to option buyers.

There are many uses for options that are beyond the scope of this book. Many books have been written about options. So I am not going to talk any further about options. Please do yourself a favor! If you want to gamble using options, go to a casino, where there are many games that offer much better odds than options and more entertainment. The bottom line is, you don't need options to hedge a DMMS position, since the market direction is not important for this system. Fluctuations are what DMMS strives on to generate gains for its portfolio regardless of market direction.

Question 12: How about using loss stops to protect your DMMS portfolio?

Answer: The answer is definitely no. The concept of using loss stops defeats the purpose of DMMS investing. Simply using stops implies timing and betting on market directions. That is more speculation than DMMS investing. Besides, using stops can drain your portfolio and your gain, if any. Loss stops are not needed in a DMMS portfolio.

Question 13: Why do you dislike using actively managed funds in a DMMS portfolio?

Answer: I have nothing personally against actively managed funds. I just don't see them as suitable investment vehicles for DMMS investing. It's a well-known fact that 75 to 85% of these thousands of funds underperform the market every year. Mutual funds are still a good way to participate in the market for most investors who cannot or don't want to be much more involved personally in the market. I explained previously in this book why these funds are not suitable for DMMS investing.

Many of these funds restrict the number of transactions. Another disadvantage is their way of distributing their capital gain, even when some shareholders did not realize such gains. Their additional costs and fees make them much more expensive than index funds. These are some of the disadvantages of these funds which are not acceptable to DMMS.

However, the most important reason is the fact they are actively managed funds. What do I mean by that? Well, as the market becomes volatile, an actively managed fund has two alternatives: to hold tight or to trade. Neither of these two alternatives is good. If the market keeps declining, the fund manager who chose to hold tight would be in deep trouble. Often beating the market is more important to the fund manager, even with great losses. Because he can excuse himself that he beat the market while the other 85% of the funds did not. While that is great for him, how can that be great for the investors?

On the other hand, the fund manager who chose to trade, most likely would be going in and out of the market trying to avoid the decline and catch the next upward move. During this process, this fund manager would be getting whipsawed, especially in a volatile market, causing his fund considerable losses even when the market goes just sideways. As a result of such whipsaws and trying to time the market, the fund would continue to underperform the market without the ability to make up for previous losses even when the market bounces back due to frequent trading.

Whipsaws and loss stops are major killers for most traders, including these fund managers. By the time the fund manager waits to confirm a trend reverse, a continuation of a trend, or a beginning of a new trend, most likely a large part of that trend has taken place, eliminating any further significant profit. This is a serious problem for an actively managed fund. On the other hand, an index fund basically mimics the market itself. It dives as the market dives, but it recovers as the market recovers. Index funds don't trade, therefore, no whipsaws and no trading costs. This is why DMMS uses only index funds, in addition, DMMS strives on market fluctuations with no whipsaws.

Question 14: what would you do if DMMS exhausts all available cash, yet the market keeps declining?

Answer: That may happen very rarely. Remember, DMMS does not guarantee its users to be correct on the market at any time. After all, DMMS always assumes the "don't know" position. So it never predicts a market move; it just follows the market. Remember, as well, a declining market is not a bad thing for DMMS. In fact, it's a great opportunity, a very rare opportunity, every DMMS investor should take advantage of it. As DMMS investors, we love equally bear and bull markets, with no preference for either one. For a DMMS portfolio, to exhaust all its cash, or all its shares when the market goes up, that means shares have been bought at very discounted prices and sold at much higher prices. Why anyone should complain about that?

In the case of a decline, remember, we start a DMMS position after an initial decline of about 30% or more. So by the time the portfolio exhausts all its cash, that would be -70% or more. The risk at that point is so low and the DMMS portfolio is fully invested. This is a great opportunity in my opinion. In addition, DMMS would also be taking advantage of market fluctuations. By the time the market recovers, the DMMS portfolio would be in a great shape. Similarly, when the portfolio exhausts its shares on the upside. Isn't it a great feeling to sell these shares at such high prices? If the market continues to advance, just adjust the neutral line and continue to use fluctuations to buy and sell according to the DMMS rules.

Just think of the buy-and-hold investor, who would be waiting miserably for the market to recover without making any money during that time. When the market recovers, the DMMS portfolio would grow considerably as the result of that steep decline, while the buy-and-hold is barely breaking even. We can certainly see the wisdom in the system as it assumes the "don't know" position and deal with all market conditions. Whether the market goes up, down, or sideways, it's truly irrelevant as long as it keeps moving both ways.

Question 15: Does it matter if the market declines or advances immediately after starting a DMMS position?

Answer: Either way the market goes first would be irrelevant to DMMS in the long term. Certainly, a decline at first may have a negative psychological effect on an investor as much as an advance in the market would have a pleasant effect. Nevertheless, any effect should only be characterized as a short-term effect. The long-term effect would not change, as the DMMS portfolio keeps compounding profit and interest regardless of which direction the market moves. It's not something anyone can control or tell where the market would move next. So if the market advances at the start, that would give the DMMS investor the opportunity to sell some shares at a good profit, which adds to the cash to be used to accumulate more shares at lower prices when the market declines. On the other hand, if the market declines immediately after the start, the DMMS investor should be grateful to be able to use 35% of its portfolio in cash to buy shares at discounted prices. Up or down is really irrelevant for DMMS.

Question 16: Does DMMS always show a profit?

Answer: Of course not, however, most of the loss might appear in the beginning. Nonetheless, the DMMS portfolio should always show much fewer losses than the market and the buy-and-hold portfolio. Therefore, the DMMS portfolio would always beat the buy-and-hold portfolio in a declining market, regardless of time. As for the intermediate and long terms, the DMMS portfolio should outperform as well the market and the buy-and-hold portfolio as DMMS compounds its gains from market fluctuations by buying at relatively lower prices and selling at relatively higher prices, and earning interest on its cash.

Question 17: How many DMMS positions a portfolio should have, and how do you manage them?

Answer: Personally, I use no more than two DMMS positions and that's plenty for many years. Definitely no need for more than three positions. Remember, we are dealing only with the general market. So that's very well diversified already. Personally, I like to use one position in the large-cap index, the SP500, and another position in the growth and aggressive over-the-counter, where most of the largest technology companies trade, the NASDAQ100. Usually, the Nasdaq is more volatile than the SP.

I simply don't advise or recommend anything to anyone. Everything I said here and in the entire book is simply intended for educational purposes by sharing my experience and thoughts in my system with my readers.

Final Note:

Imagine you go inside a small convenience store to find out that the owner of the store does not sell anything. That would be very strange, right? Yet, that's what the buy-and-hold does, and no one thinks that is strange at all or an unusual thing to do. DMMS brings to the financial world the type of investor with a trader attitude that turns the market into a business where shares are bought and sold, not stored on a shelf indefinitely.

As the blurry line between an investor, a trader, and a gambler becomes clearer and clearer throughout this book, I hope the time my readers spent reading this book would yield a financially rewarding time and a valuable experience in the financial market. While the market would continue to do what the market wants to do, as market participants, we learn to adopt a different attitude toward the market with some wisdom and less arrogance in dealing with the market in the world of the financial jungle. I am grateful to all my readers for allowing me to share my thoughts and experience with them.

With sincere gratitude,

JohnPierre LeCedre

About The Author

JohnPierre LeCedre, in addition to being an author, is a full-time trader and an investor. He has been extensively involved in the financial markets for about 29 years. His extensive experience in trading every investment vehicle from individual stocks, funds, commodities, and options, gives him a deep understanding and practical background in his views on the market.

The author's extensive and practical experience in the market is supported by a strong technical and academic background as well. He holds a Master of Science degree in electronics and computer engineering from California State University, Los Angeles. His technical ability is founded on a solid background in mathematics, statistics, and probability. After practicing engineering for years, the author became extensively involved in the financial markets. After many trials and errors, and long research and studies, he knew that to succeed in the market, it would take much more than simply guessing and speculating on market direction. He designed his trading system, the Digital Market Machine System, DMMS, taking out all the guessing and the emotional elements from the investing process. It took him months and years in perfecting his system and many rounds of hypothetical and actual testing on different markets before he finally succeeded in engineering his automated system.

Mr. LeCedre's approach to the market provides a unique and revolutionary methodology for dealing with the market. While most market participants, regardless of their sophistication level, bet on a specific market direction using various market research and analyses to form their opinions, the author built his system on the basis "don't know" approach. Such an assumption comes with a lot of wisdom and a better understanding of various market forces. Predicting the market moves involves a lot of arrogance and gambling guts by imposing one's opinion on the market. While DMMS' rules are very important, they are also very flexible to accommodate the investor's tolerance to risk. Hence, these rules are not written in stone; investors can apply these rules as they see fit in their investment objectives and their tolerance to risk.

The author turned the market into a business of buying and selling shares regardless of which way the market moves. DMMS takes advantage of the natural fluctuations of the market generated by market participants' mass psychology of fear and greed. Earthquakes don't hurt; only falling objects do. Similarly, the author thinks bear markets don't hurt; only the lack of cash does hurt during bearish times. This is the basic theory of investing using DMMS.

OTHER BOOKS BY THE AUTHOR

Words Only The Heart Says...

(Available in English and French)

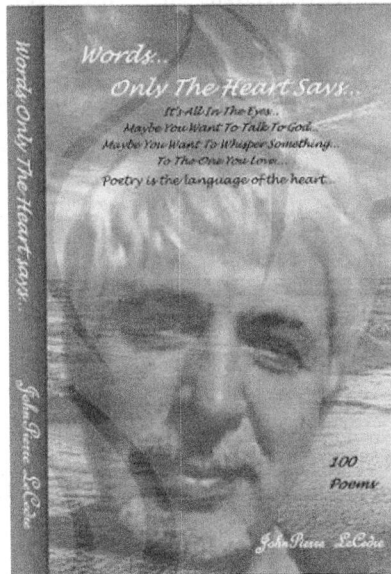

It's the eyes...
It's all in the eyes...
Maybe you want to talk to God...
Or whisper something to someone you love...
You feel it deeply...
And you fall into it helplessly...

Someone you want to love Endlessly and forever...
But even forever is not forever...
Most people eat and go...
Some leave a deep trace in the heart...
Still there...
It's in the eyes...
If you are someone who still looks ...
In the darkness of the night to the heavens...
And wonders about God and the stars...
Or you still watch the sunset and what's behind...
If the sound of water and the ocean waves...
Still, soothe your heart...
Or a beautiful love song...
Still brings tears to your eyes...
Your heart still screams in silence...
Words of love you still see in the eyes...
"Words only the heart says..."
When you are alone...
And your heart cries...
And your soul prays...
For words of love, warmth, and tenderness...
Like candlelight on a cold, dark night...
Let this melody of words...
Combine with the harmony of...
All that you feel in your heart

Poetry is the language of the hearts. Enjoy all these poems, and please leave a review to spread this joy to other people's hearts...
Thank you from the heart...
My sincere gratitude,
John Pierre LeCedre

Does G⊕D Exist?

"The Proof"

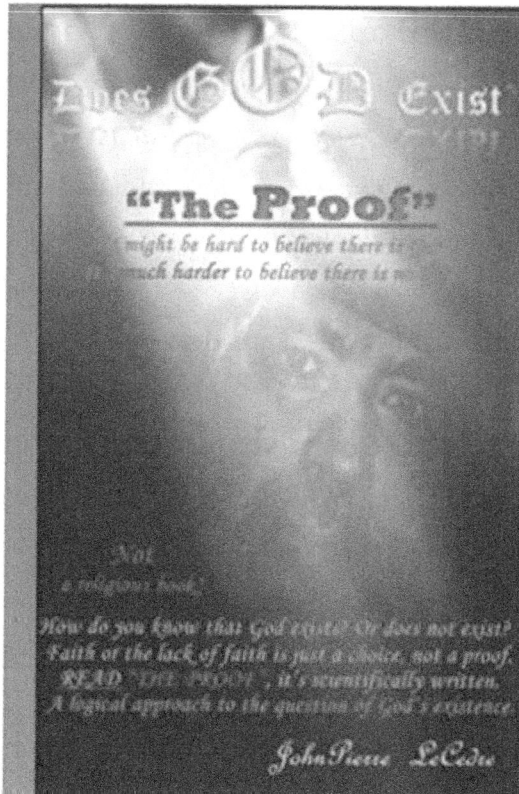

(Available in English, French and Spanish)

It might be hard to believe there is God...
*it's **much harder** to believe there is no God...*

Do you believe in God just by faith? But faith is not proof. If you are a believer, how do you know that God exists? Or if you are an atheist, how do you know that God does not exist? And if you're in between, you might not know which direction you should lean. In reality, the majority of people are agnostic and often don't know it. How do we know if what we believe is true? Is it true because society, family, church, etc. told us it is? It's mass psychology and herd mentality. The truth is not a democracy we vote on. The majority can be wrong. A thing is proven true only if the result is always the same. Is gravity real? Well, you can test it millions and billions of times. The result will always be the same. Then gravity must be true. It doesn't matter whether people believe in gravity or not; it just exists.

Does God Exist? Don't just believe he exists, or don't just believe he doesn't exist. Know the truth about God! If God exists, you would like to love him. If God doesn't exist, then you're delusional and wasting your time. Know the "true" truth about God. Faith is not proof. Read **"The Proof"**!

Does God Exist? You might ask, how do I know? Let me ask you, does darkness exist? Does ignorance exist? Does evil exist? I'm sure everyone would agree that darkness, ignorance, and evil exist in our world. My answer is that darkness exists because of the lack of light; then light must exist, since we can recognize darkness. Ignorance exists because of the lack of knowledge, then knowledge must exist since we can recognize ignorance. And evil exists because of the lack of God, then God must exist since we can recognize evil.

This is not a religious book. It is a logical and scientific approach to the question of the existence of God written by an engineer, not a priest. God and religions often have little to do with each other. I was a doubtful believer; I was also a doubtful atheist; I was always spiritually conflicted. Then I found God in such a different way. Indeed, I am still not religious and have no religious affiliation. I'm inclined to digest things analytically and logically. I want to share this logical and scientific proof with other people who are drowning in their spiritual doubts.

Often when people are asked: Does God exist? The answer would generally be "yes, no, maybe" without being able to give a logical explanation. They might try to refer to the Bible or find an unsatisfactory explanation. Faith or lack of faith is not proof. God is not a "thing" that natural laws can apply to him. If he is a "thing", he would not be God. We cannot understand God; if we can, then he would not be God. God cannot be defined; to define God is to limit him by our human minds. He is the cause of all causes without being caused. From him, all things came into existence. If you believe that after millions or billions of years everything comes into existence by chance, think again! A thing cannot create itself when it does not exist! It's like believing that your mother gave birth to herself! Absurd, of course.

I wrote this book to share my experience with any soul who wants to know God. He is absolute and eternal; he has no equals, no partners, and no comparables. He is God, the only God, the one God, the Almighty God.

My sincere gratitude,

John Pierre LeCedre

Made in the USA
Las Vegas, NV
29 January 2025